REVIEW OF THE INTERNAL ADMINISTRATION'S STUDY CRITICAL OF CLINTON DRUG POLICY AND WHITE HOUSE SUPRESSION OF STUDY

AF770892

HEARING

BEFORE THE

SUBCOMMITTEE ON NATIONAL SECURITY, INTERNATIONAL AFFAIRS, AND CRIMINAL JUSTICE

OF THE

COMMITTEE ON GOVERNMENT REFORM AND OVERSIGHT HOUSE OF REPRESENTATIVES

ONE HUNDRED FOURTH CONGRESS

SECOND SESSION

OCTOBER 1, 1996

Printed for the use of the Committee on Government Reform and Oversight

U.S. GOVERNMENT PRINTING OFFICE

45–081 WASHINGTON : 1998

For sale by the U.S. Government Printing Office
Superintendent of Documents, Congressional Sales Office, Washington, DC 20402
ISBN 0-16-055982-0

COMMITTEE ON GOVERNMENT REFORM AND OVERSIGHT

WILLIAM F. CLINGER, JR., Pennsylvania, *Chairman*

BENJAMIN A. GILMAN, New York
DAN BURTON, Indiana
J. DENNIS HASTERT, Illinois
CONSTANCE A. MORELLA, Maryland
CHRISTOPHER SHAYS, Connecticut
STEVEN SCHIFF, New Mexico
ILEANA ROS-LEHTINEN, Florida
WILLIAM H. ZELIFF, JR., New Hampshire
JOHN M. MCHUGH, New York
STEPHEN HORN, California
JOHN L. MICA, Florida
PETER BLUTE, Massachusetts
THOMAS M. DAVIS, Virginia
DAVID M. MCINTOSH, Indiana
RANDY TATE, Washington
DICK CHRYSLER, Michigan
GIL GUTKNECHT, Minnesota
MARK E. SOUDER, Indiana
WILLIAM J. MARTINI, New Jersey
JOE SCARBOROUGH, Florida
JOHN B. SHADEGG, Arizona
MICHAEL PATRICK FLANAGAN, Illinois
CHARLES F. BASS, New Hampshire
STEVEN C. LATOURETTE, Ohio
MARSHALL "MARK" SANFORD, South Carolina
ROBERT L. EHRLICH, JR., Maryland
SCOTT L. KLUG, Wisconsin

CARDISS COLLINS, Illinois
HENRY A. WAXMAN, California
TOM LANTOS, California
ROBERT E. WISE, JR., West Virginia
MAJOR R. OWENS, New York
EDOLPHUS TOWNS, New York
JOHN M. SPRATT, JR., South Carolina
LOUISE MCINTOSH SLAUGHTER, New York
PAUL E. KANJORSKI, Pennsylvania
GARY A. CONDIT, California
COLLIN C. PETERSON, Minnesota
KAREN L. THURMAN, Florida
CAROLYN B. MALONEY, New York
THOMAS M. BARRETT, Wisconsin
BARBARA-ROSE COLLINS, Michigan
ELEANOR HOLMES NORTON, District of Columbia
JAMES P. MORAN, Virginia
GENE GREEN, Texas
CARRIE P. MEEK, Florida
CHAKA FATTAH, Pennsylvania
BILL BREWSTER, Oklahoma
TIM HOLDEN, Pennsylvania
ELIJAH E. CUMMINGS, Maryland

BERNARD SANDERS, Vermont (Independent)

JAMES L. CLARKE, *Staff Director*
KEVIN SABO, *General Counsel*
JUDITH MCCOY, *Chief Clerk*
BUD MYERS, *Minority Staff Director*

SUBCOMMITTEE ON NATIONAL SECURITY, INTERNATIONAL AFFAIRS, AND CRIMINAL JUSTICE

WILLIAM H. ZELIFF, JR., New Hampshire, *Chairman*

ROBERT L. EHRLICH, JR., Maryland
STEVEN SCHIFF, New Mexico
ILEANA ROS-LEHTINEN, Florida
JOHN L. MICA, Florida
PETER BLUTE, Massachusetts
MARK E. SOUDER, Indiana
JOHN B. SHADEGG, Arizona

KAREN L. THURMAN, Florida
ROBERT E. WISE, JR., West Virginia
TOM LANTOS, California
LOUISE MCINTOSH SLAUGHTER, New York
GARY A. CONDIT, California
BILL BREWSTER, Oklahoma
ELIJAH E. CUMMINGS, Maryland

EX OFFICIO

WILLIAM F. CLINGER, JR., Pennsylvania
CARDISS COLLINS, Illinois

ROBERT CHARLES, *Staff Director and Chief Counsel*
SEAN LITTLEFIELD, *Professional Staff Member*
IANTHE SAYLOR, *Clerk*
DAN HERNANDEZ, *Minority Professional Staff Member*

CONTENTS

REVIEW OF THE INTERNAL ADMINISTRATION'S STUDY CRITICAL OF CLINTON DRUG POLICY AND WHITE HOUSE SUPPRESSION OF STUDY

TUESDAY, OCTOBER 1, 1996

HOUSE OF REPRESENTATIVES,
SUBCOMMITTEE ON NATIONAL SECURITY,
INTERNATIONAL AFFAIRS, AND CRIMINAL JUSTICE,
COMMITTEE ON GOVERNMENT REFORM AND OVERSIGHT,
Washington, DC.

The subcommittee met, pursuant to notice, at 10:10 a.m., in room 2154, Rayburn House Office Building, Hon. William H. Zeliff (chairman of the subcommittee) presiding.

Present: Representatives Zeliff and Mica.

Also present: Representatives Clinger, Hastert, and Cummings.

Staff present: Robert B. Charles, staff director and chief counsel; Sean Littlefield, professional staff member; Chris Marston, legislative assistant; Ianthe Saylor, clerk; and Daniel P. Hernandez, minority professional staff member

Mr. ZELIFF. Good morning. The hearing on the Subcommittee on National Security, International Affairs, and Criminal Justice will now come to order.

We are holding these hearings today to review a study on drug policy, a study we believe to have significant findings, prepared by an independent group, the Institute for Defense Analysis, at the request of Secretary of Defense Perry in 1994.

The basic findings of the study were submitted to the Office of National Drug Control Policy in early 1996, and while efforts were made to take some conclusions out of this study, the final draft was created in May 1996.

In terms of background, this subcommittee has oversight responsibility for our Nation's drug war and has the utmost respect for our new drug czar, Barry McCaffrey, as well as our Nation's Interdiction Coordinator, Adm. Bob Kramek.

In the course of some 19 hearings that have come before this subcommittee, the subcommittee has questioned for some time the administration's strong reliance on treatment as the key to winning our Nation's drug war, and furthermore this subcommittee has questioned the wisdom of drastically cutting to the bone interdiction programs in order to support major increases in hard-core drug addiction treatment programs.

The basis for this change in strategy has been the administration's reliance on the 1994 RAND study, and therefore we need to make sure that in the light of new major trends and increase in teenage drug use, that we continue to plan and place our resources where we can get the best results.

I would also like to mention, in terms of cooperation between both sides of the aisle, that this subcommittee has worked with the Coast Guard in transit zone programs. We have gone into the transit zone area. We held a hearing in Puerto Rico. Over the past 2 years it has accomplished an awful lot of work in refocusing the Nation on the importance of the drug war. Our first witness was Nancy Reagan, and she kind of led this effort off, but we have come a long way in getting our Nation refocused.

The Speaker of the House asked Denny Hastert and I to go to South America to visit source country programs—Mexico, Panama, Colombia, Bolivia, and Peru—to take a look at what was working and not working and come back and make recommendations to the Speaker. Denny Hastert has worked tirelessly in working with the appropriators and putting the package together. In the last 3 or 4 days, we have been able to accomplish an awful lot in terms of not only getting the drug czar his much needed staff, but to give him the resources needed to do his job.

So it has been a bipartisan cooperative effort, and again, I believe that it is a major challenge that we face in terms of the future of our country, in terms of the next generation. I don't think there is anything more important particularly when you combine crime and drugs.

Now the issue today that we will be talking about initially, is that apparently Admiral Kramek, the Interdiction Coordinator, attempted to brief President Clinton's drug czar, General McCaffrey, on the IDA study in March 1996 with two of the study's authors. General McCaffrey, whom we have tried hard to support again, and I have indicated our support for him through his complete tenure, which is approximately the last 6 months, allegedly refused to hear the briefing. This in combination with other events surrounding that refusal has left many of us on the committee troubled and confused.

Cooperation is a two-way street, and we obviously need to see all the data that comes in whether it agrees with our philosophies individually or agrees with others' philosophies. So I think it is very important that we stay on track with all the information that is available out there.

We expect to hear testimony bearing on the question of whether the study, which appears to have been highly critical of President Clinton's drug control strategy, was intentionally delayed, altered, or otherwise suppressed.

In essence the study's conclusions are two: First, source country and interdiction programs do work, although they were cut by the present administration in 1993, 1994, and 1995; and second, the RAND study justifying record level funding for drug treatment is seriously flawed. We will hear expert testimony on the study today as well.

It is not easy for those of us who have been working with, and been very highly supportive of, both General McCaffrey and Admiral Kramek to be asking some of these tough questions. On the other hand, we feel it is our responsibility in terms of oversight responsibility of our Nation's drug war to make sure we have everything on the table, everything we can possibly use in terms of measuring resources, and in our judgment, again, this is our Nation's No. 1 problem, and we need to make sure that whatever resources we have give us the best opportunity to win the war on drugs.

So as the day progresses, we hope to discover the truth about three things: First, whether the study exists, and in what form or forms, since the public does have a right to know its conclusions; second, whether it is, in fact, highly critical of the administration's strategies, specifically demonstrating the cost-effectiveness of interdiction, and documenting the failings of the RAND treatment study; and third, whether the study has been altered, delayed or suppressed in some way.

[The prepared statement of Hon. William H. Zeliff, Jr., follows:]

Opening Statement of Chairman Bill Zeliff
Hearing of the Subcommittee on National Security, International Affairs and Criminal Justice
"Review of Internal Administration Study Critical of Clinton Drug Policy,
and White House Suppression of Study"
October 1, 1996

We are holding these hearings today to review a study of drug policy, a study we believe to have significant findings, prepared by an independent group, the Institute for Defense Analysis, at the request of Secretary of Defense Perry in 1994.

The basic findings of the study were submitted to the Office of National Drug Control Policy in early 1996 and while efforts were made to take some conclusions out of this study, the final draft was created in May 1996. Admiral Kramek, the Interdiction Coordinator attempted to brief President Clinton's Drug Czar, General McCaffrey, on the study in March of 1996 with two of the study's authors. General McCaffrey, whom we have tried hard to support through his tenure, allegedly refused to hear the briefing. This, in combination with other events surrounding that refusal, has left many of us on the committee troubled.

We also expect to hear testimony bearing on the question of whether the study, which appears to have been highly critical of President Clinton's drug control strategy, was intentionally delayed, altered, or otherwise suppressed. In essence, the study's conclusions are two. First, source country and interdiction programs work, although they were cut by the present administration in 1993, 1994 and 1995. Second, the RAND study justifying record-level funding for drug treatment is seriously flawed. We will hear expert testimony on the study today as well.

It's not easy for those us who have been highly supportive of Gen. McCaffrey and Admiral Kramek to be here asking tough questions today. On the other hand, even in a political season--perhaps, especially in a political season--we must be faithful at all times to the truth.

We hope to discover the truth about three things today:
First, whether this study exists and in what form or forms since the public has a right to know its conclusions; Second, whether it is, in fact, highly critical of the administration strategy, specifically demonstrating the cost-effectiveness of Interdiction and documenting the failings of the RAND treatment study; and Third, whether the study has been altered, delayed or suppressed in some other way.

Mr. ZELIFF. I would like to turn to Mr. Cummings from Maryland for his opening statement.

Mr. CUMMINGS. Thank you very much, Mr. Chairman.

On the eve of the adjournment of 104th Congress in exactly 5 weeks before the election, we are participating in the 18th hearing this subcommittee has held on the important issue of illegal drugs in our Nation. Unfortunately, the very title of this hearing, "Review of the Internal Administration's Study Critical of Clinton Drug Policy and White House Suppression of Study," suggests just another partisan attack on the administration's drug policy shortly before the election.

Mr. Chairman, I believe that there are several important points that need to be made. First, the subject of this hearing, a draft report by the Institute for Defense Analyses on the cost-effectiveness of interdiction programs, is just that. We are having a hearing on a draft. The final report has yet to be issued. Both you and I know that draft reports from many Government entities are frequently subjected to reworking after the draft has been circulated for comments.

The Office of National Drug Control Policy received a copy of this draft report in May of this year. The ONDCP sent the draft to five independent specialists to conduct peer review analysis. None, I repeat none, of the five reviewers were paid for their services. In a further attempt to ensure a balanced review, the five reviewers were anonymous so they could feel free to write what they thought about the report without any chance of outside pressures exerting influence over their findings. Almost all peer reviews conducted by academic journals are anonymous.

What did the panel reviewers discover? One peer reviewer stated that: Empirically the study is flawed by a failure to interpret a number of data series correctly. Overall the panel was unanimous, and I repeat unanimous, in its conclusion that the report is seriously flawed and is in need of substantial rewrites before the study can be published in final form. Remember, this is a draft study that we are discussing here today, the same one that I just said was unanimously determined to be flawed.

The panel of peer reviewers were not the only ones who had problems with this draft study. Officials within IDA itself have expressed concern about the draft report. According to a July 10, 1996 IDA memorandum, serious questions were raised about the validity of the draft report.

For the record, I would like to point out that IDA has made the first three pages of this July 10, 1996, memorandum available to both the majority and the minority. This memo from Ralph Richanbach agrees that the methodology in this draft report is flawed, but we are going to have a hearing today on a flawed draft. He states: The only relevant issues are whether or not there are price increases at the retail level and whether these price increases can be correlated in time with specific interdiction events. Even if this correlation can be found, additional work must be done to demonstrate a causal relationship.

Mr. Richanbach goes on with a detailed analysis of the problems in the study.

Mr. Chairman, at this point I ask unanimous consent that the July 10, 1996, memo from IDA be included in the hearing record.

Mr. ZELIFF. Without objection so ordered.

[The information referred to follows:]

IDA

July 10, 1996

MEMORANDUM TO: Tom Christie

FROM: Paul H. Richanbach

SUBJECT: "An Empirical Examination of Counterdrug Program Effectiveness" (IDA Document D-1837) and Its Critics

Summary and Conclusions

This paper seeks to answer one basic question: Do domestic retail cocaine prices move in response to specific source-zone interdiction campaigns? The authors believe they do. The anonymous reviews (forwarded by John Carnevale of ONDCP) raise a number of methodological issues that call into serious question the validity of this conclusion.

The centerpiece of the IDA analysis is a newly constructed series for the price of cocaine. This price series is flawed by the averaging of retail and wholesale prices. It must be revised to include only retail (less than 5 grams?) prices. If the authors are correct that the inclusion of wholesale prices has no effect on the resulting price series, then (a) the results will still stand , and (b) this is a curiosity which should be relegated to a footnote or appendix. *The only relevant issues are whether or not there are price increases at the retail level, and whether these price increases can be correlated in time with specific interdiction events.* Even if this correlation can be found, additional work must be done to demonstrate a causal relationship.

Several analytical excursions need to be eliminated from the paper. The construction of demand elasticities is absolutely unnecessary. The mistakes and controversies surrounding this part of the work are nothing but a distraction. If the authors wish to make a contribution to this area of research, they should do so in another paper. The same holds true of the projection of the price floor using an exponential decay function. It is both nonsense and unnecessary. Take it up in another paper.

Both the authors and the reviewers fail, however, to ask a second basic question: If so, so what? Do *transitory* increases in price affect cocaine consumption in the long term or the number of users (prevalence) in either the short or long term? It seems improbable. Not only must the authors demonstrate that interdiction increases prices, but they must further show that this has some *permanent* effect on prevalence and/or consumption.

Conclusion: Fix the price series. If the results are the same, claim the correlation, but be more modest about the causation and look for other supporting data. Eliminate all unnecessary analyses—in particular demand elasticities, projections of the price floor, and the claim that the difference between the projected and observed price floors is attributable to the interdiction campaigns.

The Model

A clear failing of the IDA paper is the lack of a well-articulated model of the dynamics of the cocaine market, of how supply disruptions might work their way through this market, and of the goals of an anti-drug policy. In fact, the model used by IDA has, *inter alia,* the following (implicit and explicit) features, all of which must be satisfied in order for their argument and conclusion to hold:

1. Discrete interdiction operations in source-zone countries have a large and immediate impact on the total supply of cocaine available for distribution in the market.

2. Because inventories of cocaine are small relative to the size of the entire market, these source-zone supply disruptions have a large and immediate impact on export prices (or on import prices in the U.S.).

3. The distribution channels for cocaine in the United States are characterized by mark-ups along the supply chain that are multiplicative, rather than additive; i.e., large increases in cost at one level result in proportionally large increases at (all) subsequent levels.

4. Significant increases in the retail price of cocaine are observed that correlate in time with discrete interdiction operations, and for which there are no other known explanations.

5. Significant increases in retail prices result in significant decreases in quantities consumed and the number of people who use cocaine (prevalence), in both the short and long runs

6. Transitory price increases could be made permanent if the discrete events that caused them (the interdiction operations) were themselves made permanent, rather than transitory.

Detailed Comments

1. *The impact of source-zone interdiction enforcement on supply.* This seems highly plausible, but the authors offer no quantitative evidence of this assertion; e.g., estimates of cocaine exported from South America. Furthermore, no effort has been made to hold the effects of source-zone interdiction campaigns constant for all other possible explanations. For example, several reviewers agree that prices rose substantially in 1990. They postulate that this was, at least in part, due to the successful law enforcement campaign against the Medellin cartel (the result of which might have been a temporary disruption in supplies) and the increased power of the Cali cartel after the fall of the Medellin organization (which might have resulted in greater monopoly power and an ability to raise prices to extract greater profits), and to other law enforcement successes in Panama and Mexico at about the same time.

2. *Inventories and export (import) prices.* One of the reviewers indicates that this is an industry in which there are substantial inventories. If so, this would obviously dampen the price impact of any supply disruption. If inventories are not large, then the

impact of supply disruptions would be felt more quickly. Which is it? This is an empirical question, but if there is no consensus, then the issues as they appear in the literature must at least be framed, and their implications assessed. Furthermore, the obvious place to look for this price impact would be on export and import prices. Again, this is an empirical question; reference must at least be made to the current amount and quality of data and level of understanding of this issue.

3. *Mark-ups*. If the wheat in a $1.00 box of cereal costs 5 cents, and the price of wheat doubles, the box of cereal will increase in price by about 5 cents. (The exact amount depends primarily on the degree of competitiveness at all stages of the supply chain, and on the competition between grain-based cereals and substitute products). The IDA authors assume that the mark-ups in the cocaine trade are not additive, but multiplicative. Thus, a 50 percent increase in the import price of cocaine will result in a 50 percent increase in the retail price. This may be right, but it would be unique, particularly for a product market that appears to highly competitive. What does the literature have to say about all this, and on what basis does the IDA analysis make similar or contrary claims?

4. *Retail price increases*. Here the debate over the IDA analysis is confused by the introduction of unnecessary—either overstated or just plain silly—arguments. The only important issue is whether or not the price series constructed by the IDA authors is valid.

The reviewers are quite correct to take the IDA analysis to task for failing to distinguish between retail and wholesale prices in using the STRIDE data to construct their price series (Figure 1, page 6). Because unit price decreases with the quantity purchased, the use of quantities above normal retail transactions (5 grams according to one reviewer) *must* have the effect of lowering the calculated prices. The introduction of non-retail price data into the retail price calculations invalidates the entire series.

Furthermore, even if there is shown to be a correlation between price increases and specific interdiction campaigns, causation has yet to be demonstrated. What role did other events that occurred at these same periods in time have on the observed price movement? How much of the 1990 price increase may be due to the bringing down of the Medellin cartel, the expanded power of the Cali cartel, and other events in Panama and Mexico in 1990 (as the reviewers have suggested)? Were there other events in this and other years that might have contributed to price increases? How much, if any of the correlation is caused by source-zone interdiction, and how much is caused by other factors?

The first thing I learned in my first econometrics course is that *correlation does not imply causation*. (The first thing I learned in my first statistics class was the golden rule of statistics: "tell me what you want to prove and I will prove it for you.") Economics students are cautioned repeatedly not to go "data mining." One must have a theoretical basis, an underlying model, for trying to understand causal links, and it is that theoretical construct or model that one tries to verify or reject with the available data and evidence.

Having said this, the basic method employed by IDA makes sense to me. If the pattern of price increases holds true when the price series is properly constructed, then the IDA analysis may be very important.

It is a distraction to invent new economic theory and assert unheard of economic empiricism by declaring that the price floor for cocaine (after 1989) can be projected from past prices on the basis of an exponential decay function. And it is unnecessary, since the literature will support using a price close to that which is needed to make the authors' argument. (The floor price, if it could be predicted, is a function of marginal cost and the degree of monopoly power that can be exercised in the market.)

It is equally distracting to pick a fight about the effectiveness of domestic law enforcement activities. To say these activities have had no effect on price is both wrong—the effect is embedded in the cost of doing business, and therefore the price of the product—and overstates the simpler, though still debatable point that these activities (if thought of as a long term, steady state level of activity) cannot explain sudden changes in price.

In particular, the reviewers are quite correct in noting that the IDA analysis offers no evidence in support of the assertion that source-zone interdiction explains any of the difference between the projected price floor ($25) and the observed price floor (slightly more than $50). *If* one believes that the observed price floor is higher than some other, hypothesized price floor—a point I am unwilling to concede until I see more convincing evidence—then one might further hypothesize that the difference may be due to the effect on the cost of business imposed by law enforcement activities, or it may be due to the exercise of market power by oligopolists. Or it may be due to source-zone interdiction campaigns. Who knows?

The IDA price series is in nominal, not real dollars. This must be corrected. Among other things, the flat, dotted line price floor of about $50 would in fact be decreasing from 1989-1996 if the series were deflated.

5. *Price increases, consumption, and prevalence.* Significant price increases will, everyone agrees, result in significant reductions in consumption. Whether the demand elasticity for heavy users is -0.3, -0.5, or -1 is of little consequence here. The IDA attempt to construct demand elasticities is unnecessary. There is no reason not to use the elasticities developed by others and available in the literature—especially since the differences between them would have no appreciable effect on the outcome of the analysis.

Unfortunately, many of the reviewers comments on the subject of price elasticities seem valid. In particular, the IDA analysts show no apparent understanding of the distinction between movement *along* a demand curve and the movement *of* a demand curve. This is the identification problem raised by several reviewers; it is one of the first things taught in econometrics classes, and is thus the kind of rookie mistake that unnecessarily undermines the credibility of the rest of the analysis.

A final problem here is that because any price increases are transitory—I continue to discount the alleged affect on the price floor—the effects on consumption must also be transitory. (I suppose one could argue that temporarily high prices might prevent someone from becoming a user, or might push someone over the edge to becoming a non-user, but such effects must be quite small.) So what is the point of the interdiction campaigns?

Suppose that by temporarily increasing the price of cocaine, consumption is reduced by half (e.g., the price doubles and the elasticity of demand is -0.5). I could easily posit a behavioral model that suggests the following: many heavy users, with very inelastic demand, simply spend whatever income they have on as much cocaine as their money will buy. There may be little or no decrease in the ***number*** of heavy users. If a notional casual user consumes 1 gram per month, but cuts back to 1/2 gram per month due to the price increase, the number of users still remains the same. How much better off are we if consumption decreases but prevalence remains the same? What are our social goals? What effect do various attempts at supply and demand reduction have on long term consumption versus prevalence, and which is to be more valued? In short, what is the correct behavioral model? Are there other reasons to engage in interdiction operations that have little to do with their effect on prices; e.g., support for democratic institution-building in source countries, or reinforcement of the social unacceptability of drug use among young people and other potential users?

6. *Making interdiction operations permanent.* Perhaps the point is that these transitory price increases need to be made permanent by making interdiction operations permanent? If so, consider the implications of reversing this logic: if we are not prepared to undertake interdiction operations that will make these price increases permanent, then there is no value to conducting them in the first place. Unless their effects can be made permanent, there is no discernible long run effect on consumption.

cc: Barry D. Crane
A. Rex Rivolo
Gary C. Comfort

Mr. CUMMINGS. Thank you, Mr. Chairman.

Finally, I am troubled by accusations from the majority that the administration has somehow tried to bury this draft study. During his last appearance before us, General McCaffrey, who, by the way, I have utmost respect for, answered questions about the IDA report and made it clear that, first, he believed the initial draft of this report to be flawed; and, second, that neither he nor anyone else in the administration wanted to suppress the report.

In a September 20, 1996, letter to Chairman Zeliff, General McCaffrey sent the results of the peer review panel, making it clear that if ONDCP had wanted to suppress this draft, he would not have ordered peer review analyses.

Mr. Chairman, every one of us on this panel knows that General McCaffrey's integrity and reputation is above reproach. I am disappointed that General McCaffrey has to appear before us today to answer these unfounded charges of covering up the IDA draft report. I know that General McCaffrey could be spending his time more wisely, much more wisely, in confronting the drug problem. In fact, he could be in my home city of Baltimore where the drug problem is severe.

Mr. Chairman, I admire and applaud your commitment to fighting this scourge of drug abuse in our Nation. I repeat my offer to you to assist you in any way. However, finding a solution to the drug problem must be bipartisan and free of election-year politicking. People are dying. Interdiction is an important component to ending the drug problem.

I am almost finished.

I do not oppose interdiction programs; however, we must not forget treatment and prevention. As General McCaffrey has stated on numerous occasions, all three of these elements must work together if we are to make real progress in ending the supply of illegal narcotics in the United States.

In closing, let me welcome back General McCaffrey and Admiral Kramek. I also look forward to hearing the testimony of our witnesses today.

Thank you, Mr. Chairman.

[The prepared statement of Hon. Elijah E. Cummings follows:]

Statement of
Hon. Elijah E. Cummings

Subcommittee on National Security, International Affairs and Criminal Justice
October 1, 1996

Thank you Mr. Chairman. On the eve of the adjournment of the 104th Congress and exactly five weeks before the election, we are participating in the 18th hearing this Subcommittee has held on the important issue of illegal drugs in our nation. Unfortunately, the very title of this hearing, "Review of Internal Administration Study Critical of Clinton Drug Policy and White House Suppression of Study," suggests just another partisan attack on the Administration's drug policies shortly before the election.

Mr. Chairman, I believe there are several important points that need to be made. First, the subject of this hearing, a draft report by the Institute for Defense Analyses (IDA) on the cost-effectiveness of interdiction programs, is just that -- a draft. The final report has yet to be issued. Both you and I know that draft reports from many government entities are frequently subjected to re-working after the draft has been circulated for comments.

The Office of National Drug Control Policy (ONDCP) received a copy of this draft report in May of this year. ONDCP sent the draft to five independent specialists to conduct peer review analyses. None of the five reviewers were paid for their services. In a further attempt to ensure a balanced review, the five reviewers were anonymous, so they could feel free to write what they thought about the IDA report without any chance of outside pressures exerting influence over their findings. Almost all peer reviews conducted by academic journals are anonymous.

What did the panel of reviewers discover? One peer reviewer stated that quote "Empirically, the study is flawed by a failure to interpret a number of the data series correctly" end quote. Overall, the panel was unanimous in its conclusion that the IDA report is seriously flawed and is in need of substantial rewrites before the study can be published in final form. Remember, this is a draft study that we are discussing here today.

The panel of peer reviewers were not the only ones who had problems with this draft study. Officials within IDA itself have expressed concern about the draft report. According to a July 10, 1996 IDA memorandum, serious questions were raised about the validity of the draft report. For the record, I would like to point out that IDA has made the first three pages of this July 10, 1996 memorandum available to both the Majority and Minority.

This memo, from Mr. Paul Richanbach, agrees that the methodology in this draft report is flawed. He states quote "The only relevant issues are whether or not there are price increases at the retail level, and whether these price increases can be correlated in time with specific interdiction events. Even if this correlation can be found, additional work must be done to demonstrate a causal relationship" end quote. Mr. Richanbach goes on with a detailed analysis of the problems in the study.

Mr. Chairman, at this point, I ask unanimous consent that the July 10, 1996 memo from IDA be included in the hearing record.

Finally, I am troubled by accusations from the Majority that the Administration has somehow tried to bury this draft study. During his last appearance before us, General McCaffery answered questions about the IDA report and made it clear that one, he believed the initial draft of this report to be flawed and two, that neither he nor anyone else in the Administration wanted to suppress the report. In a September 20, 1996 letter to Chairman Zeliff, General McCaffery sent the results of the peer review panel, making it clear that if ONDCP had wanted to suppress this draft, he would not have ordered the peer review analyses.

Mr. Chairman, every one of us on this panel knows that General McCaffery's integrity and reputation is above reproach. I am disappointed that General McCaffery has to appear before us today to answer these unfounded charges of covering-up the IDA draft report. I know that General McCaffery could be spending his time more wisely in confronting the drug problem. In fact, he could be in my home city of Baltimore, where the drug problem is severe.

Mr. Chairman, I admire and applaud your commitment to fighting the scourge of drug abuse in our nation. I repeat my offer to you to assist you in any way however, finding a solution to the drug problem must be bi-partisan and free of election-year politicking. Interdiction is an important component to ending the drug problem. I do not oppose interdiction programs. However, we must not forget treatment and prevention. As General McCaffery has stated on numerous occasions, all three of these elements must work together if we are to make real progress in ending the supply of illegal narcotics in the United States.

In closing, let me welcome back General McCaffery and Admiral Kramek. I also look forward to hearing the testimony of our other witnesses.

Thank you Mr. Chairman.

Mr. ZELIFF. Thank you Mr. Cummings, and I am well aware of your commitment to this very important issue. I will just read the last paragraph of that three pages you just inserted in the record. Having said this, the basic method employed by IDA makes sense to me. If the pattern of price increases holds true, and the price series is properly constructed, then the IDA analysis may be very important. But we will discuss this as we go through the hearing.

I would like to now turn to the chairman of our full committee, Mr. Clinger from Pennsylvania, for his opening statement.

Mr. CLINGER. Thank you very much, Mr. Chairman, and I want to thank you very profoundly for calling this important hearing, and I want to tell you what I believe is important in all of this. Two things are important: The process and substance.

On the process I have to tell you that whether or not the IDA, Institute for Defense Analyses, study is the best study or worst study done is not the issue. We are going to hear about the accuracy and findings of the report and whether or not it deserves to be given credence or credibility.

But that really isn't the issue. The issue is that it needs and deserves to be part of the debate, part of the discussion as we went into the appropriations process this year. What matters is that it was a year-long internal administration study that came to conclusions that were, at the very least, uncomplimentary of the Clinton drug strategy between 1993 and 1995, and the drug czar, we are told, was unwilling, refused, to even take a briefing on the study.

Let me just indicate that to me it seems a very flawed process that leads to having the top White House drug policy official, the gentleman for whom we have all indicated we have enormous respect, to, for whatever reason, whether from pressure from elsewhere or whatever, to reject out of hand a study on the basis of its conclusions without at least hearing from the distinguished and eminent scientists and Ph.D.'s who wrote it.

Process point No. 2: There is a lot of talk going on around here and elsewhere about cooperation now. I think we would all welcome and applaud cooperation and the fact we are told that the administration wants to cooperate with Congress to restart—because I think we would all agree that the war has been in limbo for some time—to restart the effort to deal with drug menace in this country.

But I think we really have to make the record very straight. This committee, this subcommittee, has held 19 hearings on drug policy starting in March 1995, as Chairman Zeliff said with Nancy Reagan, and this committee has been trying to engage the administration on drug policy from the beginning. This President gave seven major addresses in 1993 and 1994 and mentioned drugs zero times. He gave more than 1,600 interviews and speeches in 1993 and mentioned drugs only 13 times. In 1994, he gave more than 1,700 interviews and speeches that mentioned drugs only 11 times. This is not leadership, and this is not really giving the kind of attention to an issue that is so deadly and so threatening to the youth of this Nation.

We went through the whole appropriation process, and this, I think, is what really ultimately is my bottom line and concerns me, one in which the administration asked for record levels of spending on treatment programs and still has kept interdiction below its 1991 and 1992 levels. This study's conclusions would have helped immeasurably to advance that debate. At the very least, the conclusions and the recommendations should have been part of that debate. If they could be disproven or found not to be valid, that is one thing; but the fact that they weren't even considered weren't even on the table for discussion is a serious disappointment.

Members of this committee have met four or five times with General McCaffrey privately, and I must say, I am advised he never once mentioned this study's existence or its conclusions or its recommendations, which would have at least confirmed the need or at least suggested the need to reverse the administration's priorities. This is not cooperation.

If we are going to have cooperation now, we are grateful for that; but we have not had, in my view, cooperation in the past. We never got a chance when it would have counted to debate this study's merits or discuss openly the seemingly misguided priorities of the White House in 1993, 1994 and 1995, and we could have done so effectively with this study on the public record.

I think the point is that this study, as in all studies that are done with regard to this menace, needs to be a part of the public record and part of public debate. The study would have bolstered what the designated Interdiction Coordinator Admiral Kramek wrote to former drug czar Lee Brown in December 1994. He stated then that—I am quoting—"we must return to 1992–1993 levels of effort" in interdiction. Yet no action was ever taken as a result of that warning that Mr. Brown issued at that time. This White House has effectively deprioritized interdiction in order to pump billions into more treatment. We are not saying treatment doesn't need to be part of the mix, but I think that the imbalance between the resources devoted to treatment and those devoted to interdiction is seriously askew.

So the result, direct or indirect, of failed leadership and a failed interdiction strategy has been a dramatic rise. We have seen the evidence of that in the studies that are out most recently the STRIDE data of last week, the dramatic rise in drug availability, in purity, increased use, increased incidence of use, a drop in price and frightening increase in use and drug abuse.

So again, Chairman Zeliff, I want to applaud you and the members of your subcommittee who have been so persistent and tenacious in pursuing this issue when, frankly, we were not seeing the kind of commitment and tenaciousness from the other end of Pennsylvania Avenue. You stepped out in front on this issue in a tireless effort to bring about change, and I commend you and all the members of this subcommittee, Mr. Mica, Mr. Hastert, and others who have taken such a great leadership role in this area.

Mr. ZELIFF. Thank you, Chairman Clinger.

[The prepared statement of Hon. William F. Clinger, Jr., follows:]

Good morning. I want to thank the chairman for calling this hearing, and I want to tell you what I believe is important in all this. Two things are important -- process and substance.

On the process, I will tell you that whether the IDA study is the best study ever done or the worst study ever done is really not the issue. That debate strikes me as secondary. What matters is that it was a year-long, internal Administration study. It came to conclusions that were, at the very least, uncomplimentary of the Clinton Drug Strategy between 1993 and 1995. And the Drug Czar refused, we understand, to even take a briefing on the study. Let me say that it is a flawed process that leads the top White House drug policy official to reject out of hand a study on the basis of its conclusions, without at least hearing the PHDs who wrote it.

Process point number two. There is a lot of talk going around about cooperation now, and how the Administration wants to cooperate with Congress to restart the drug war. Well, let's get the record straight -- This subcommittee held 19 hearings on drug policy, starting in March of 1995 with Nancy Reagan, and this committee has been trying to engage the Administration on drug policy from the beginning. This president gave 7 major addresses in 1993 and 1994, and mentioned drugs zero times. He gave more than 1600 interviews and speeches in 1993, and mentioned drugs only 13 times. In 1994, he gave more than 1700 interviews and speeches and mentioned drugs only 11 times. That is not leadership.

On this report, let me tell you what bothers me. The Drug Czar refused a briefing on it in March of 1996. But Congress never even got the chance to hear these conclusions -- and we would not be here today, except for the courage of one of the 19 people who had one of the limited edition, control-numbered, laser-tabbed copies. That is not how the process of cooperation works.

We went through the whole appropriation process, one in which the Administration asked for record levels of spending on treatment programs, and still has kept interdiction below its 1991 and 1992 levels. This study's conclusions would have helped immeasurably to advance that debate. Not having them is a disappointment.

We met 4 or 5 times with General McCaffrey privately, and he never once mentioned this study's existence or its conclusions -- which would have confirmed the need to reverse the Administration's priorities. That is not cooperation.

We never got a chance, when it would have counted, to debate this study's merits or discuss openly the seemingly misguided priorities of the White House in 1993, 1994 and 1995, and we could have done so effectively with this study on the public record. I need only remind this audience that Admiral Kramek wrote a letter to the former Drug Czar in December 1994 stating, in relevant part, and I quote "we must return to 1992-1993 levels of effort" in interdiction. That internal letter described the fact that an agency head consensus believed we were on the cusp of a national security issue in the Administration's approach to the drug war. Yet no such action was ever taken.

Only this year, without this study to back the effort up or any assistance from the White House, did the Republican Congress get the drug war back on track. We have agreed to exceed the President's request for funds by more than $280 million. Only now, in the eye of a presidential campaign have we gotten any response.

That I think brings us here today. On the topic of drug interdiction and the source country programs, I am sure we will hear a lot today about what new initiatives the Administration has underway. What we will not hear is the background for all this new talk.

We will not hear that the Republicans in Congress, many of them sitting right here, worked hard to exceed the President's request with $165 million for Defense Department participation in Interdiction, $46 million for DEA including agents on the ground in the source countries, $42 million to put 3 more P-3 aircraft up, $28 million to enhance Customs efforts, and another 300 INS officers on the border.

In essence, let's get the facts. We have not had cooperation until now, 1996, and it is a little bit late in the game. The White House has not had a priority on interdicting drugs prior to their getting to this country; and we have put $3 billion into treatment programs that have generated little if any progress in the drug war. The opportunity cost has been a rise in drug availability and purity, a drop in price, and a dramatic increase in youth use. That cannot stand, and this is just the latest chapter in the Administration's attempt to explain away a major policy failure.

Mr. ZELIFF. Another gentleman that I have already mentioned that has done heroic work in terms of appropriations committees, working on behalf of the Speaker in terms of assisting the subcommittee as we went to South America and tried to pull the programs together, Denny Hastert from Illinois.

Mr. HASTERT. I thank the chairman. It is interesting to come before this committee today and ask some important questions about our drug policy. I don't view this—I am not a chairman of any committee or any subcommittee, but I have been around this place for 10 years, and I see one of the basic threats to our security and to our children is drugs in this country.

I guess I wear a couple of different hats coming here. First of all, I come in here as a father, a father that hopes my teenage sons don't get embroiled in any type of drug use, that they don't have to go through any types of programs.

I guess I come also into this committee room with the old academic hat of an economist. I am not an economist with a Ph.D., but I did my major work in economics, and I taught economics in a high school for 16 years, and one of the basic things we talked about economics are where trends coordinate; where prices are high, there must be reasons for high prices. When demand is low, there must be reasons for that low demand. When things disrupt the ordinary process of somebody coming from market to—or from manufacturing to the final market, it was all kinds of things can interfere.

And I think it is relevant, contrary to the gentleman from the other side of the aisle, from Baltimore, I think, when you find those disruptions and those parallels, there should be an honest attempt to understand why they happen, not just to gloss them over or just say, well, there is something wrong with the science.

When we talk about science in these types of surveys, sometimes Congress gets too embroiled in studies. It is right that we do studies, and it is right we understand why things happen and to go beyond just testimony or the talk that we have going between ourselves and this—on this dais from time to time and the testimony we get from expert witnesses, but to go out in the real world and find out why things really happen.

So the other hat that I bring on in this thing is somebody who has been asked by our leadership, and I am part of the leadership, to try to help where we think there needs to be shoring up, especially in things like appropriations, and going out in the source countries and seeing what happens, to see that there are real programs going on, and people are doing real things out there to stop; because we can talk about abstract places, faraway places like the jungles of Bolivia, or the Amazon Basin in Peru, or the jungles of Colombia, or Panama or even Mexico. That is something that is beyond most of our experience. We don't know what goes on there, or the cultural situations there, or the reason the campasinos are trying to make a living for their families or how they do that. We don't know the interaction of our DEA agents and military and other people who are trying to work with organizations on the ground in those countries. But when you are there and see it, you literally see people risking their lives day in and day out on a foreign soil, and some of those being foreign nationals, to try to make life better in this country, then we owe those folks, and we owe those people the ability to make sure that they can get their job done and what the priorities of that job should be.

So when I go around, as I have been tasked to do, and talk to the chairmen of various appropriation committees and saying, boy, can we get some money into this bill so we can get the P3 on the ground or off the ground or into these source countries, so that we can see what the drug-flying drug trade is with down-looking radar, or can we fix some spray planes in Colombia or in Mexico so that we can deliver herbicides to this death threat, whether it has poppy fields that create heroin or whether it is the cocaine plant fields that deliver coca and crack to our streets and to our children; and when I find a member or a chairman of my own party of an appropriation committee that somewhat sanctimoniously waves in my face a study done by the RAND Corp. a couple of years ago saying that the RAND study shows that there is no link at all between interdiction and most of the drugs in the street. For that reason I am not going to put money in the Coast Guard or interdiction because this study tells me something else, then we find evidence that there is evidence to the contrary.

Contrary to my good friend from Baltimore, it is not a draft, it is a final draft, and a final draft has been denied distribution because what apparently seems a political purpose, a political purpose that is there to justify a policy by the White House long before my friend General McCaffrey ever came to be the drug czar, but to justify something that causes teenage drug use to double, that causes 12th graders to use more drugs than we have ever had used by this population, that is actually poisoning the youth of this country.

Come on. We need to get down to all the reasons this happens, and if we have good information that is done on some scientific basis that we can use to justify putting funds into interdiction as well as funds into the demand side, the treatment programs that we have—but again it shouldn't be all one way or all the other.

The commonsense approach this Congress is trying to take in the last 2 years is to find what are the reasons for things happening, whether it is health care, Social Security, or Medicare, and then when we find those reasons, let's apply common sense to that reason and make sure that we have things in place that make interdiction work. Things that hold down the cost of drugs or drive up the cost of drugs and hold down demand so that at least maybe 150,000 or 200,000 of our kids can't afford this, or it's not within their scope of recreational purposes, that kind of makes sense.

So let's get the facts out. There is no place in this Congress or on a bipartisan basis or in this country to tilt the story one way or the other without really getting the facts.

So I welcome this hearing today. I hope we get down to the facts. I can understand just some little things we are able to do. For instance, we stress that we have worked hard to give this administration what it has asked for and more. We put $165 million more in counternarcotics than in the defense bill, and it just happened because this administration wanted that to happen. We put $20 million more for DEA than the President's requested in the first place. Other people said we needed to have this. We put $75 million more in DEA agents for the source countries and more in virtually every area that's been highlighted.

So we, through the evidence that we found, have tried to help the situation, and we have given the drug czar—General McCaffrey will be here today—an extra $60 million in discretionary funds so he can use that money to best decide how he can fight the drug war without politics pulling on him from one side or the other.

Now we also need to find out what works and what doesn't work; where we need to put these resources, and where we don't need to put these resources. If we can't have honest answers and people bringing forth honest information, then shame on us and shame on this Congress. And I yield back.

Mr. ZELIFF. Thank you, Mr. Hastert. I would just like to quickly echo one comment in terms of your opening statement. There was a lot of conflicting evidence on source country programs when we decided to make that trip down there. In a very short 6 days, we were able to sort out a lot of that conflicting evidence, and working with everybody's involvement in the drug war, we came back with many recommendations that we discussed with the drug czar and both sides of the aisle in your efforts in even the last 3 or 4 days in getting the funding that they need. I think very much there has been a very strong bipartisan effort.

The gentleman from Florida, Mr. Mica.

Mr. MICA. I thank the chairman for calling this hearing's and all the hearings' attention to this national problem that is destroying our youth and many of the productive citizens of our country. I also thank him for agreeing to my request for this hearing because I think it is important that this matter be investigated.

I call for this hearing because of really two reasons. First, I was dumbfounded when I learned that the first act of our drug czar may, in fact, have been to bury a report that had critical information, that was a conscientious report. Second, I was most concerned when I learned that there was attempted intimidation of others to keep this report from the Congress and the American people. Those are the two reasons why I asked for this report.

I am not the only one that has called for an examination of what this administration's policy or lack of policy is. In fact, I think you wrote to the President, Mr. Chairman, not too long ago, and you quoted the Wall Street Journal where our FBI Director and DEA Director said, "Last spring"—this is from that article—"Last spring Federal Bureau of Investigation Director Louis Freeh and DEA's Mr. Constantine wrote a scathing memo to Mr. Clinton warning that the administration's drug strategy was dangerously adrift"—not my words, their words.

Then we have a report that, in fact, details of the failure of this policy—let me tell you the rest of why I called for this hearing. I learned from a source close to the report of certain facts that were brought to my attention. First of all, the damning conclusions of this—and this is a nonpolitical—it is not a Republican, it is not a Democrat, it is a nonpolitical, and, in fact, it is an empirically rigorous assessment which was commissioned not by me, not by this committee, but by those at the very top of the administration—was, in fact, intentionally buried and may have been done so as the first act of our new drug czar.

The authors of the study presented their conclusions in person to the new drug czar in the company of others—and we will hear from some of those folks today—early this year. When the new drug czar learned the conclusions, he instructed that the study be quashed.

Incredibly, the report's existence—and again I repeat what my colleague just said, this is its final draft. I had—as a member of this committee, I just got a copy of this, in fact got it from the press before I got it officially, but this has been quashed since May of this year, and actually from March when it was originally kept secret.

What further concerns me is that the new drug czar thereafter knowingly embraced the same treatment, reduced interdiction and source country level prevention priorities in the President's 1996 White House Drug Strategy that were set by President Clinton in 1993, 1994, 1995.

In summary, the White House knowingly quashed its own rigorous but damaging study in an election year because that study showed the failure of the Clinton policies in the prior 3 years. It also showed detailed cost of that failure, and there was a quantifiable increase in the number of drug users and annual drug-related deaths, and I think the evidence of that report is very clear.

What concerns me is not just that this report has been suppressed and buried and now kept until maybe after the election, but let me show you in my community what has been done. This is the headline from the Orlando Sentinel, July 14, 1996: "Long Out of Sight, Heroin is Back Killing Teens."

I come from a very peaceful, suburban, prosperous area in central Florida. That is what is going on. This is the headline in my paper this past Sunday, a week ago Sunday: "Orlando Area Teen Drug Use Soars." As a parent, as a Member of Congress, as a concerned American and someone who is not a Johnny-come-lately on this, I asked for hearings. In fact, I had over 100 Members bring a signed letter to the former chairman of this committee begging for a hearing about a policy we knew was sending the children in this country down the tubes, and that hearing was denied, and I was gaveled out of order in this very room because no one wanted to pay attention to that problem. So we have seen what has taken place.

Now I am concerned about what I have heard that has taken place in this study. We see the results in my neighborhood, not just in Baltimore, but all across this land, and we need to make sure that this whole drug abuse problem, that the attention given by this administration and everyone in Congress is a priority.

Thank you, Mr. Chairman for your leadership.

Mr. ZELIFF. Thank you Mr. Mica.

At this point I would like to welcome our first panel. These three gentlemen authored the report we are discussing today. They come from the Institute of Defense Analyses. Dr. Gary Comfort is the assistant director of the operational evaluation division of IDA. Drs. Rivolo and Crane are research staff members of the operational evaluation division.

Thank you for being here, gentlemen. With that, I would ask you to come forward. Please raise your right hand.

[Witnesses sworn.]

Mr. ZELIFF. Let the record show that the question was answered in the affirmative.

We would like, if you would, to, perhaps each of you, give your opening statements, condense them. The balance of your opening statement, written statement, can be accepted for the record, but if you would kind of condense it and fit it into approximately 5 minutes or so.

Mr. COMFORT. Mr. Chairman, we did provide a statement to the committee staff yesterday and requested that it be placed in the record.

Mr. CLINGER. Pull that microphone a little closer to you.

STATEMENTS OF GARY C. COMFORT, ASSISTANT DIRECTOR, OPERATIONAL EVALUATION DIVISION, INSTITUTE FOR DEFENSE ANALYSES; BARRY D. CRANE, RESEARCH STAFF MEMBER, OPERATIONAL EVALUATION DIVISION, INSTITUTE FOR DEFENSE ANALYSES; AND A. REX RIVOLO, RESEARCH STAFF MEMBER, OPERATIONAL EVALUATION DIVISION, INSTITUTE FOR DEFENSE ANALYSES

Mr. CRANE. I am Mr. Barry Crane, project leader for the counterdrug effort. To my right is Dr. Rex Rivolo, the principal analyst, and to my left is Dr. Gary Comfort. We are pleased to have this opportunity to clarify the content and status of our report.

The principle objective of our research has been to examine the effectiveness of source-zone interdiction activities upon cocaine supply in the United States; based upon that examination, to suggest strategies and operational activities to increase effectiveness.

We believe that the central finding of our report is that a well-conceived source-zone action has directly resulted in significant increases in the street price of cocaine in the United States, and, through market impact, of price upon demand, and resulted in decreased consumption of cocaine. We have found that effective source-zone activities can be conducted at a relatively modest funding level, and, therefore, that well-conceived source-zone operations can be more cost-effective than has been previously acknowledged.

I don't mean to imply that all operations are necessarily cost-effective. One can pursue ineffective strategies and tactics in the source zone just like anywhere else. But our research indicates that activities that significantly and unexpectedly disrupt the established coca distribution channel will rapidly produce real effects on the streets of the United States.

The major purpose of a draft document is the stimulation of dialog, the examination of hypotheses, and the receipt and consideration of constructive criticisms. That process is ongoing. We believe that the final report that will result from this process will incorporate a number of clarifications while retaining the findings we believe are central to the research.

We believe our research has been of assistance to those responsible for planning and executing source-zone interdiction efforts, and we expect the final report that results from the ongoing review process will be a useful tool to motivate and assist the planning and execution of additional cost-effective source-zone actions.

That is our opening statement, sir.

[The prepared statement of Mr. Crane follows:]

JOINT STATEMENT OF GARY C. COMFORT, BARRY D. CRANE, AND ARTHUR R. RIVOLO TO THE SUBCOMMITTEE ON NATIONAL SECURITY, INTERNATIONAL AFFAIRS, AND CRIMINAL JUSTICE

This statement is provided in response to requests from the Subcommittee.

Gary C. Comfort is an Assistant Director of the Operational Evaluation Division at the Institute for Defense Analyses (IDA). Barry D. Crane and Arthur R. Rivolo are Research Staff Members in the Operational Evaluation Division at IDA.

The Institute for Defense Analyses operates a federally funded research and development center established to assist the Office of the Secretary of Defense, the Joint Staff, the Unified Commands, and Defense Agencies in addressing important national security issues, particularly those requiring scientific and technical expertise. IDA takes great pride in the high caliber and timeliness of its analyses, produced in an atmosphere that encourages independent thinking and objective results.

The Principal Deputy Assistant Secretary of Defense for Special Operations and Low Intensity Conflict oversees the Drug Enforcement Policy and Support (DEPS) program for the Department of Defense. Under a task order from that office and related tasking, IDA carries out a number of research activities addressing demand control programs and interdiction activities supporting the Department of Defense and the U.S. Interdiction Coordinator. These include assessment of military drug testing and control programs; evaluation of the performance of the relocatable over-the-horizon radar network; assessment of capabilities to monitor illegal air transport of drugs throughout the source and transit zones; maritime and riverine interdiction performance; evaluation of proposed technological improvements to enhance DoD counterdrug capabilities; and the provision of quarterly performance evaluations to the Interagency Planning Conference. Dr. Barry Crane serves as the project leader within IDA for these research activities.

As one element in support of the DEPS tasking, the study team authored a draft document entitled "*An Empirical Examination of Counterdrug Interdiction Program Effectiveness*." In accordance with established long-standing procedure, a draft of this document was provided to the task sponsor and other offices approved by the task sponsor in May 1996. Consistent with the objectives of a draft document, this on-going process of review and critique has produced thoughtful comments from a substantive number of reviewers, both internal to IDA as well as from outside reviewers. We are now well along in the process of carefully evaluating each of the many comments received. We anticipate that the final report that will result from this review process will incorporate a number of substantive clarifications while retaining the findings that we believe are central to our research. The remainder of this statement will discuss the scope of our research work underlying the subject study, the methodologies employed in that research, and the findings from that research that we believe are the primary contributions of our work.

In execution of the task order, consistent with our operational orientation and experience, we adopted an approach of examining the data describing actual operational experience with drug trafficking and drug usage without requiring *a priori* theoretical models of how drug trafficking and drug use *should* respond. Toward this end, the IDA study team collected extensive data bases made available by DoD elements and the numerous other agencies involved in combating drugs or in accumulating related data. Such data included known and suspected drug trafficker routings and flight tracks from the source-zone countries through the transit zone, drug price and purity data maintained by the Drug Enforcement Administration, and surveys on drug use collected by Health and Human Services.

Because these data bases contain large numbers of dispersed events, each of the data bases is necessarily "noisy," *i.e.*, they contain many entries that are non-representative "outliers." We employed straightforward data processing and analysis methodologies in the examination of these data bases in order to extract meaningful trends from noisy statistics. In particular, we developed a cocaine street price index defined as the median unit price for the pure cocaine content of all DEA transactions smaller than 10 kilograms. This is not unlike the consumer price index computed from a representative "market basket" and used to monitor the economy.

One of the major cocaine data bases is that maintained by the Drug Enforcement Administration as the *System to Retrieve Information from Drug Evidence* (STRIDE) program. The STRIDE data base includes the price and purity of many thousands of actual or negotiated street buys by DEA agents. This data base comprises the "market basket" from which our street price index is computed. After processing the STRIDE data base, we noted that our cocaine street price index since 1985 is characterized by a smoothly decreasing trend on which is superimposed a number of distinct, but short duration, upward excursions or "bumps," which seemed to beg for an explanation.

We noted that these perturbations corresponded in time with the initiation of several specific source-zone interdiction activities. Consequently, we formed the hypothesis that well-conceived supply disruption activities in the source-zone countries can produce significant excursions in the price and purity of cocaine in the U.S.

At the quarterly meeting of the Interagency Planning Conference in May 1995, we argued that the air bridge between the growing regions in Peru and the processing in Colombia was a weak link in the drug trafficking distribution network. At the August 1995 meeting, we recommended strong action to sustain interdiction against the air bridge. We predicted in open forum at the December 1995 meeting of the Interagency Planning Conference that the shoot-down policy that had been initiated during 1995 by the government of Peru had so disrupted the air bridge for coca product transport from Peru to Colombia that, when STRIDE data for the ensuing period became available, our trend processing would reveal an increase in the U.S. street prices for cocaine of 30 to 50 percent. When the STRIDE data for the relevant period became available, our prediction was confirmed. This result greatly increased our confidence that the correlations we had observed between source zone events and street price index excursions were causally related.

In January 1996, we briefed Admiral Kramek, in his capacity as the U.S. Interdiction Coordinator, regarding the consistent correlation we had observed between the implementation of source-zone supply disruption activities and perturbations in the STRIDE data, including the predicted response to the shoot-down policy. At this time, we conveyed a sense of opportunity for capitalizing on this market disruption. Admiral Kramek indicated that he believed our results were of significance and called a special meeting of The Interdiction Committee (TIC) to be briefed on our findings. The TIC members advised Admiral Kramek that we collect the next few months of STRIDE data for further confirmation before sponsoring our results to the White House.

Our task sponsor, however, did arrange a staff level discussion with key staff from ONDCP in late January 1996. Among other suggestions offered at that discussion, a key ONDCP staff member questioned our assumed price-demand elasticity, *i.e.*, the marketplace linkage between price changes and the consumption of drugs. Based on that discussion, we appended the basic document to include our findings linking price index to several data bases that are logically related to drug usage. These data bases included the SmithKline-Beecham Clinical Labs data on random drug testing in the workplace; the

45-081 98 - 2

Department of Health and Human Services Drug Warning Network (DAWN) data base on emergency room treatments related to cocaine; and the Department of Justice Drug Usage Forecasting (DUF) data base from quasi-random testing of arrestees in major cities. Again, we employed straightforward analytical techniques to extract trend data with the maximum possible resolution. We noted that perturbations in these drug usage indicators corresponded in time with the perturbations in the STRIDE price data, *i.e.*, when price went up, the drug usage indicators went down, *etc.* From these correlated changes we determined initial estimates of the price elasticity of demand.

Throughout this research project, we kept the sponsoring office of our task order informed of our emerging results. Our research showed significant effects on street prices directly affecting cocaine usage as a result of several source zone initiatives that had been conducted with relatively modest expenditures. Our sponsor recognized that this apparent cost-effectiveness of source-zone activities conflicted with the findings of a previously published study entitled "*Controlling Cocaine*" that found source zone activities were the least cost-effective of the four cocaine control strategies considered. The most cost-effective of those strategies, treatment of heavy users, was found to be some 23 times more cost-effective than a source-zone interdiction strategy. Our task sponsor asked that we expand our analysis efforts to explain the apparent large differences in our emerging findings regarding the cost-effectiveness of source zone interdiction efforts and those presented in *Controlling Cocaine*.

Consequently, we undertook a review of *Controlling Cocaine*. We found that, in our opinion, *Controlling Cocaine* had underestimated the effects of major coca production disruption in the source zone by using a measure of effectiveness that overly relied on quantity of drugs seized. Since routine drug seizures in the source zone can be readily compensated for by the drug traffickers via increased drug production, in the steady-state, source-zone drug seizures are little more than a cost of doing business. We also found that the demand model used in *Controlling Cocaine* failed to reproduce the actual demand data for the years for which data were available from the National Household Survey on Drug Abuse. Finally, we observed that the cost-effectiveness projected for the treatment strategy in *Controlling Cocaine* was inconsistent with the data on treatment expenditures and the resulting number of treatments actually experienced during 1992-1996.

We documented our analysis outlined above in a draft IDA document, *An Empirical Examination of Counterdrug Interdiction Program Effectiveness*. As noted on the inside cover of that document, an IDA document is used for the convenience of the sponsors or the analysts to make available preliminary and tentative results of analyses. We believed, and continue to believe, that our central findings are of significance and that the timely discussion and understanding of those central findings can assist in motivating, guiding the planning for, and evaluating the results of effective source zone operations. In our view, the central findings of our research are the following:

- STRIDE data can be used to assess the effectiveness of source-zone activities and to provide useful feedback to those executing such source-zone interdiction operations.
- Well-conceived source-zone operations that significantly and unexpectedly disrupt the normal drug trafficker processes for producing and transporting coca products from the source-zone cause discernible increases in the street price of cocaine in the U.S. and, through normal market relationships between price and demand, thus reduce cocaine consumption.

Consequently, we believed the release to our task sponsor of a draft document was an appropriate mechanism to make our research results available to the drug control community in a timely manner while at the same time inviting and recognizing the need for the review and critique of our draft by others. As discussed above, we believe that such a review and comment process is proceeding and that the final report that will emerge from this process will continue to support the central findings.

As the authors of this document, we are concerned that some of the findings contained in our draft that we consider of lesser significance to our overall research may have been presented in a manner that invites misinterpretation. Specifically, we have made no assessment of the appropriate emphasis to be placed upon supply control programs versus demand reduction programs. Since interdiction efforts are the focus of our research, we have not examined either law enforcement or treatment programs to an appreciable extent, and we have made no claims as to the value of those strategies within an overall drug control program.

Our draft report does contain a figure that graphically depicts the cost-effectiveness of specific supply control and demand reduction strategies. However, a full reading of the text makes clear that the cost-effectiveness that is depicted for source country control "is only directly applicable to the experience of 1995." Further, the cost-effectiveness depicted for treatment is not the result of an independent, in-depth analysis by IDA of the costs and effectiveness of treatment. As identified in the text of the document, the estimate of treatment cost-effectiveness utilizes the data extracted from *Controlling Cocaine*, with the exception that, rather than using the increased number of treatments projected in *Controlling Cocaine* with an increasing expenditure for treatments, we instead used the number of treatments and the expenditure for treatments as actually experienced in 1995.

We will endeavor to present our central findings and other findings with clarity in the final report so as to reduce the potential for misinterpretation.

Mr. ZELIFF. Either of you gentlemen have opening statements?

Mr. COMFORT. No, we don't, Mr. Chairman.

Mr. ZELIFF. I guess one quick question I would have in just starting, and I have been involved with a corporate career as well as a small business, and as well as being in Congress here, and you say this is a draft, and it is ongoing, and apparently this is not a final draft?

Mr. CRANE. Let me clarify the way IDA manages its process. A substantial document, as you see in the front cover of the report, goes through a much more strenuous review process. The purpose of our draft is to get out our initial findings for comment and review to strengthen it. It is a very important aspect of the scientific process to give and receive criticism. We asked for strong criticism, and the purpose of that is to clear up misconceptions, errors in exposition or even faulty reasoning, but in this case we do need to make some improvements in exposition.

Mr. ZELIFF. I guess my problem here is how many drafts are you into now? What number is this one?

Mr. CRANE. This is the only one marked "final." It was intended for distribution internal to the inner agency.

Mr. ZELIFF. How many drafts preceded the final?

Mr. CRANE. Just three, sir. If you look, this is what we call a slant four, and this is the fourth draft. We did receive others.

Mr. ZELIFF. The idea is the Defense Department contracts you to go out and do a study; you come back and present the results of the study; then you get asked to keep changing it?

Mr. CRANE. No, sir, we didn't get asked to keep changing it. We receive criticisms, we evaluate them, and continually improve the report. The criticisms we received, for example, from ONDCP are extremely valuable criticisms. They do not change the central thesis, but will greatly increase our ability to communicate those findings effectively.

Mr. ZELIFF. You haven't changed the basic philosophy of the report. The basic conclusions of the report still remain the same from the beginning to the end?

Mr. CRANE. Yes, sir, for the most part that is true.

Mr. ZELIFF. For the most part. And you stand by your original conclusions?

Mr. CRANE. The primary conclusions that the source-zone operations are highly effective, we stand by those.

Mr. ZELIFF. And what about the RAND study?

Mr. CRANE. We believe that we had obtained substantial data. We tried to understand certain aspects of the cocaine market. We matched that data to the methodology of the RAND study, and the conclusion we came to is that we could not follow the analysis of that study because the data didn't—contradicted RAND's approach.

Mr. ZELIFF. Let me see if I hear you right. You couldn't follow the analysis of the study, so does that mean that the study was flawed?

Mr. CRANE. There are like any other study——

Mr. ZELIFF. Let me be more specific. You couldn't follow the analysis of the study, therefore—we are referring to the RAND study of 1994, which basically has a heavy emphasis on treatment, and thereby we made decisions to cut back interdiction. I am asking you is the study, in your judgment, flawed, the conclusions of that RAND study of 1994?

Mr. CRANE. The conclusion that the source-zone—I will be specific here because there are many conclusions. The primary conclusion, that source-zone interdiction activities were very ineffective—that is, it would cost $783 million to change consumption 1 percent—versus treatment, we found that not to be true.

Mr. ZELIFF. So, I guess the question is why I think it is important, and why we value the importance of the work that you have done here. If we are going through a false premise that treatment of hard-core drug addicts is the key to the future of the drug war, then we—and as a result of that false premise, we have cut back in a major degree interdiction, source country programs as well as transit zone programs, then we have got to make some adjustments and change direction, I would think, or at least in balance; would you agree with that?

Mr. CRANE. It is really the objective of our work to present the analytical findings. There are certainly other reasons for treatment, and I would defer that to those making decisions on how to allocate resources and so on to those who make them. We present our findings that it is less cost-effective than previously had been known.

Mr. COMFORT. Mr. Chairman, could I just suggest that the majority of our work is based upon the review of actual data. The majority of the RAND study is the presentation of models as to how the system works. What our conclusion found was that in several cases we were unable to match the actual data to the models of the RAND study. You can look for a number of reasons to possibly explain those discrepancies, but we believe that the data are what the data are.

Mr. ZELIFF. I guess the last question, I will ask it a different way. Was the RAND study model flawed, in your opinion?

Mr. COMFORT. In selected cases it does not match the data, and as a result, since we believe the data speak for themselves, we have to say that in some cases, for example, in the question, which I know is central to some of your thoughts, of the cost-effectiveness of treatment being so much less than the cost-effectiveness of source-zone interdiction, our data showed that source-zone interdiction, when carried out from well-conceived operations, can be much more cost-effective than had been modeled by the RAND study.

Our data took the RAND study's numbers for treatment as presented in their document. We just substituted for the projected number of treatments that would result from increasing the expenditures before the actual data that was available to us for the actual expenditures and treatments in 1995; and we found that led to a much lesser cost-effectiveness than what RAND had modeled. That does not in itself speak to the cost-effectiveness of treatment. It just says that what we saw in the actual data did not fit the RAND projections.

Mr. ZELIFF. Obviously this is a sensitive subject because people have strong feelings, and many decisions have been made as a result of the RAND study. Backing up from that, did you, as you presented your study, and you have gone through some drafts here, you say three drafts, and you apparently had a final draft here yet to be disseminated, but has anybody tried to convince you to change your thinking and take out the information on the treatment and deemphasize that in any way?

Mr. COMFORT. Mr. Chairman, I personally—I have kind of been the inside author in that I stay in the office, and these other gentlemen have been doing the interacting.

Mr. ZELIFF. My time has run out. I would like to turn it over to Mr. Hastert from Illinois. I am sorry, excuse me, my buddy from Maryland.

Mr. CUMMINGS. I do exist. I am not a potted plant over here. Thank you, Mr. Chairman.

Mr. ZELIFF. With all due respect, I apologize.

Mr. CUMMINGS. Do many of you all—there are several comments about General McCaffrey and somebody suppressing this report and all of this kind of thing. Did any of you all brief him, and who would have said that, any of you all? You heard the testimony; did you not?

Mr. CRANE. Yes, sir.

Neither of us briefed General McCaffrey.

Mr. CUMMINGS. None of you, OK.

Let me ask you something. There is an internal report, the IDA report, and there are several things—it is very critical. Your own internal report is very critical of this whole draft. How do you all respond to what is said in that report?

Let me just point out one thing very quickly. On page 3 of this analysis, it says, "the first thing I learned in my economics course is that correlation does not imply causation", and then it goes on. How did you all respond to that?

Mr. RIVOLO. Let me respond to that, Mr. Cummings. First of all, I would like to point out that in addition to that one critique, we had five others which say this a wonderful piece of work, publish it.

Mr. CUMMINGS. May we have that, please?

Mr. RIVOLO. Certainly, absolutely.

The arguments that are presented in this paper came after the issues were raised at ONDCP, I believe, and we looked for an economist because the work really did not involve an economist, and since we have a very good economist, we sent it to him for review. He came back with that very scathing review.

We since then interacted for a very long time, for at least 2 weeks, almost on a daily basis, whereby we went item by item and explained what was done. He has since modified his views, and if you were to bring him up and ask him, you might get quite a different situation from that original review.

Notwithstanding what I just said, the basic criticism is that the report does not address the scientific work in an economist's point of view. I am not an economist. I am a physicist. I look at the market as a physical system. I could care less about economic models. All I look for is cause and effect, if I can prove it. If I need some economic piece of application theory or procedure, I go and look for that.

We have looked at much of that. After looking at most of it, I decided that I did not need any of it to make the statement. And I must say that the nature of this document, as was alluded to by my colleague, is really one to convey information without backup evidence. We never—we never said that this document should be a stand-alone, self-sufficient document. This document coalesces about 2 years of work, very extensive work, into a few pages. You cannot do everything. The reason was that we believed that the results were very important and should become part of the discussion for the strategy.

I might, at this point, take the opportunity—I don't have a fancy, glossy figure, but I do have some data presentation which essentially outlines our entire arguments, if the member could——

Mr. CUMMINGS. I would like to have that, but let me move on if you don't mind.

One of the things that has risen here lately—not lately, but in my community—is crack cocaine. Crack cocaine is very cheap. Tell me how that played into your report. I am just curious because most—I won't say most, but a lot of people, young people that are addicted, are on crack cocaine. Tell me how that figured into all of this.

Mr. RIVOLO. Yes, sir. Crack cocaine is just another form of cocaine except that it addresses the very bottom end of the distribution machinery in that it is sold in very small quantities at very high prices, I might say. The price of crack is cheap, because the quantities are cheap, and you can afford to buy a single piece of rock, which may contain as little as 20 milligrams. That is why it is cheap.

Mr. CUMMINGS. On the other hand, it is a very addictive drug and quickly addictive; is that correct?

Mr. RIVOLO. I can't address the addictive——

Mr. CUMMINGS. In answering my question, I think you have to address that in some kind of way because although it is cheap, there is—a lot of it is needed, and I base that upon my neighborhood in talking to people on crack cocaine. It is highly addictive, and people—and based upon what you just said, it comes in small quantities, and because it is so addictive, they need a lot of it. So take it from there. I just want that to be a part of your statement.

Mr. RIVOLO. That may very well be the case. However, in looking at the industry and market as a whole, crack cocaine was folded in with all other forms of cocaine. That was just a different delivery system, and the reasons why crack cocaine appears can be addressed, and at some point if you wish me to, I can do that. But the distinction between crack and other forms of cocaine, in my opinion, is artificial, and as far as a monitor on the market, they all should be lumped in together.

Mr. CUMMINGS. Would you comment on whether you briefed others on the draft report? I think someone said this is the fourth draft.

Mr. RIVOLO. Yes, sir.

I would like to point out that the first inklings of what we were looking at happened very early in 1995—February or January. We were starting to brief the interdiction community, that is the DEA, U.S. military, Customs, those people, with this concept that there may be a better way to monitor what their effectiveness is by looking at market dynamics rather than seizures. It was very clear from the beginning that seizures are irrelevant, useless indicators, and we can show you evidence why we believe that. Once this material arose, we believe that the significance of it was worth distributing, and we distributed it. We talked to DEA and Customs extensively. We made trips to South America. We talked a great deal to agencies in Washington. We talked to CNC. We tried to promulgate this information at that time very early on, about the same time.

At about the same time, there was a discussion that Peru was about to implement a major new strategy. That strategy was one that we had already identified as extremely, extremely effective, if it was indeed implemented, and that if Peru proceeded with that implementation, that within 6 months we should see street prices rising significantly.

This piece of data which I distributed is essentially the evolutionary history of that statement. By September 1995, many individuals besides us—and I might refer you to an article in the New York Times dated September 15, 1995, in what officials described as the most precipitous shift in almost 6 years, the wholesale price of cocaine has increased nearly 50 percent since May, while retail prices have gone up 30 percent.

We believed that way before that report came out. There were other articles at the time. Various DEA police task forces across the country were saying: What is going on here?

We knew fully well what was going on and we were trying to promulgate it. Right about that time, the RAND reports were released and we diverted our attention from presenting this logic and this methodology to essentially analyzing the RAND reports and they were a large digression, which took a lot of time, Mr. Cummings.

Mr. CUMMINGS. Just one more question, please, Mr. Chairman.

You just said something that really kind of struck me. I want to make sure I understood you. You said the seizures were irrelevant or are you saying that as a part of this report information about seizures is irrelevant? I'm just curious.

I just want to make sure. Because this committee has spent a lot of time on interdiction. I just want to make sure I understand what you are saying. That's all.

Mr. RIVOLO. Yes, sir. The canonical measure of effectiveness has always been seizure, the seizure rate. In looking at the technical implications of that, we quickly see that seizures correlate with availability. That is, when there are a lot of drugs on the market, seizures are very high. When there is none, seizures are very low. And, therefore, to try to measure success with something which goes up and down with availability, is counter, and we dismissed that very early on.

We came to the conclusion that the amount of material seized does not affect the market, and when you back that up by other studies, for instance, that production capacity is about 30 times the current production, it tells you if the market has to expand by 30, 40 percent for seizures, it does so and it does so very quickly.

In fact, if we increased seizures, increase to the cost of operations would be very small, because I might remind you that the cost of production for cocaine is about $1 per gram. And if you double it or triple it, it's still fairly a small amount of money to lose if the final product sells for $15,000—$15 a gram, and ultimately on the streets for $100 and $150.

So our analysis came to the conclusions, and we stand behind it and we like to debate in the open, that seizures is a very poor indicator, and one of the criticisms of the RAND report in our report was that that was used as a gauge of the effectiveness of treatment versus interdiction.

Mr. COMFORT. Mr. Cummings, if I could point out regarding seizures, that our study has primarily looked at what causes disruptions to the ongoing price trends so that we have been interested in what causes those price trends to change over fairly short amounts of time. Clearly underlying the overall price trend, seizure has its place. It certainly increases the cost of doing business to those who are trafficking in drugs and certainly adds something to their costs which wind up being some addition to the street prices.

Our point is that in the shorter term, with the more dramatic effects on pricing, we don't see that seizures make a big—is a good indicator to tell you you are doing things correctly.

Mr. ZELIFF. The gentleman from Illinois, Mr. Hastert.

Mr. HASTERT. I thank the chairman.

Mr. Rivolo.

Rivolo; right?

Mr. RIVOLO. Rivolo, sir.

Mr. HASTERT. Rivolo.

I want to very quickly take up two followups on the questions from the gentleman from Maryland, if you could answer them. Let me lay this out and you tell me whether it's right or wrong.

To take the last question, that seizures in this country, whether you are finding something in a false bottom of a semitrailer truck or a camper that goes across I–80 and goes through Illinois in my district, for instance, there is so much substance in the pipeline that a seizure here and a seizure there really hasn't affected what the market price of that product is. Is that what you said?

Mr. RIVOLO. I must clarify it. Seizures in the United States, once the material has been run through the machinery, is very valuable. And loss of that material costs the machinery a great deal of money and, therefore, it's felt.

However, it's immediately replaced. There is no obstruction—people think that we can affect the supply. We cannot affect the supply. The supply is the——

Mr. HASTERT. That is, seizures on the high sea or seizures in airplane?

Mr. RIVOLO. Those are less valuable. They are much less valuable because the product doesn't cost much, leaving Colombia at $1 a gram. If they lose a few tons, it is no big deal. They just replace it. It is a nuisance cost of doing business, and they account for that in their pricing structure.

Mr. HASTERT. Let me go back to the first question the gentleman asked.

He asked you, basically, in my understanding, if there is a—not the seizures but a disruption in the pipeline, if the shoot-down policy in Peru, for instance, or the situation where you interdicted a large logistical node, at the San José del Guaviare in Colombia, that made a difference and that type of strangling the pipeline showed empirical evidence at the end that the cost of that product went very high as compared when there is no disruption in the pipeline. The cost, as the gentleman said on the streets of Baltimore for crack cocaine or any type of cocaine, is very cheap. Is that correct?

Mr. RIVOLO. What is very cheap? The——

Mr. HASTERT. If there is no disruption in the pipeline, the cost of that product on the streets of Baltimore is cheap, relatively cheap?

Mr. RIVOLO. There is a very elaborate distribution chain at which the value of the material increases rapidly by going through about 4 or 5 steps. At each step, the value increases.

Mr. HASTERT. I am talking street price. It is basically very simple.

Mr. RIVOLO. OK.

Mr. HASTERT. If the street price in Baltimore is cheap, that means there probably hasn't been a disruption in the pipeline along the way; is that correct?

Mr. RIVOLO. That's is correct. Basically——

Mr. HASTERT. When there is a disruption in the pipeline, when you squeeze down the ability of drugs to move out of Colombia or you break down the transportation system between Peru and Colombia, then eventually along the line it shows a rise in the price, is that correct, on the street?

Mr. RIVOLO. If the transportation pipeline is interdicted, not poking holes in it by seizing it, because that can easily be replaced, if you interfere with the normal transportation or production mechanism, which is strongly dependent on one mode, you will immediately have a shortage produced because it's not a matter of replacing it.

Mr. HASTERT. I don't want too much information. I just want an understanding here.

So basically you can stop the transportation, if you squeeze down the pipeline, then you raise prices. And if prices are high on the street, purity becomes low and sometimes the ability for people to buy, especially for recreational use, is somewhat impaired; is that correct?

Mr. RIVOLO. That is correct.

Mr. HASTERT. OK. So there is a relevance there. And that is basically the whole background for your study, is it not?

Mr. RIVOLO. That is correct, sir.

Mr. HASTERT. All right.

Mr. Rivolo, let me ask you, you are the principal author of this report; is that correct?

Mr. RIVOLO. I am not the principal author, but I am the analyst. I did the analytical part.

Mr. HASTERT. All right. You spent a year doing the analysis and beginning back in December 1994; is that correct?

Mr. RIVOLO. Yes, sir.

Mr. HASTERT. And the IDA has in the past, then, been critical of the Defense Department, correct, in some cases, for instance, on the B–2 bomber and the Osprey program?

Mr. RIVOLO. There have been many times where IDA's position has conflicted with the sponsor, yes, sir.

Mr. HASTERT. All right. Now, I want to make a point. Your report was sponsored by the IDA; right? That's who basically you work for and put out the report.

Mr. RIVOLO. The sponsor is the Secretary's office, sir.

Mr. HASTERT. So actually the Secretary of Defense asked you to do this study?

Mr. RIVOLO. The Assistant Under Secretary for Drug Policy, yes, sir.

Mr. HASTERT. Fine. Now, I want to take up two important issues with you. I want to remind you that certainly you are under oath, as you know, and sworn to tell the whole truth to this congressional panel as you personally remember it, no matter how difficult that may be to you.

Before I get into the substance of your report, the internal memo surrounding that report and the conclusion of that report, which suggests interdiction is cost-effective and that the administration's RAND study is unsound—let me start with a different matter. The high volume—well, when you went to brief the head of ONDCP, you said that you had never briefed the drug czar; is that correct?

Mr. RIVOLO. That is correct.

Mr. CRANE. I answered that, sir.

Mr. HASTERT. OK. But you were about to brief the drug czar; is that correct?

Mr. RIVOLO. We were asked by Admiral Kramek to take the briefing or its important conclusions to the drug czar directly, yes, sir.

Mr. HASTERT. So when you were about to brief the drug czar, after some type of a meeting, you were told that the briefing was no longer necessary; is that correct?

Mr. RIVOLO. At the time of the briefing, we were brought to ONDCP by Admiral Kramek, and I believe one or two other staffers, and the intent was to brief the general.

Mr. HASTERT. Now the ONDCP, tell me where is that?

Mr. RIVOLO. It's up on 4th Street or 5th Street.

Mr. HASTERT. It's part of the White House?

Mr. RIVOLO. It's just very close to the White House.

Mr. HASTERT. All right.

Mr. RIVOLO. We came in with a prepared briefing. We sat down. General McCaffrey came in, asked to be prebriefed by Admiral Kramek.

Mr. HASTERT. Right.

Mr. RIVOLO. They went into a room. We were expecting it to be about 5 minutes. It took about 30 minutes. They came out and Admiral Kramek relayed to us that the general did not want to hear our briefing and that in the following days' presentation, which we were to brief the interagency, that some discussion of supply and demand should not take place.

Mr. HASTERT. Now, let me get this straight, if you would indulge me for a minute, Mr. Chairman.

When I was raising my young sons, who are now older, sometimes when I was telling them something, I found out that they put their hands over their ears, that they didn't want to hear it, with the presumption if you didn't hear it, you didn't have to understand it and you didn't have to behave. Was this somewhat what happened here?

Mr. RIVOLO. I don't want to speculate on what the motivation was.

Mr. HASTERT. I understand.

Mr. RIVOLO. I know what happened, and basically, he did not want to listen to the work, for whatever reasons, and he left.

Mr. HASTERT. Now, let me ask you another question.

I understand—this was just relayed to us. You are the people who were there. Now, you were standing basically outside the door waiting to go in and do the briefing; is that correct?

Mr. RIVOLO. Yes, sir.

Mr. HASTERT. Did you overhear any of the conversation in the other room?

Mr. RIVOLO. No, sir. You couldn't hear anything.

Mr. HASTERT. You couldn't hear anything at all?

Mr. RIVOLO. You heard elevated voices once or twice, but there was no way you could understand.

Mr. HASTERT. Were they shouting?

Mr. RIVOLO. Elevated.

Mr. HASTERT. Excitement?

Mr. RIVOLO. I think the meeting was an excited one, but, we were not in there.

Mr. HASTERT. Thank you.

I will yield back.

Mr. ZELIFF. The gentleman from Florida, Mr. Mica.

Mr. MICA. Mr. Rivolo, you went there, though, with the intent of briefing the drug czar?

Mr. RIVOLO. Yes, sir.

Mr. MICA. That was your purpose?

Mr. RIVOLO. Yes, sir.

Mr. MICA. And you said you got into the room; you put your papers out and then you were asked to leave?

Mr. RIVOLO. No, we never got into the room.

Mr. MICA. You never got into the room?

Mr. RIVOLO. We were sitting in the waiting hall, waiting for General McCaffrey to come. He came in. He waved Admiral Kramek in. Admiral Kramek came out and said he wants a prebriefing, give me the slides. He took my slides. They went in and we sat outside for the duration.

Mr. MICA. And it's your understanding—now, you were told to stand or wait outside, and you said you heard elevated voices. Was Kramek yelling at the drug czar?

Mr. RIVOLO. I don't know who was yelling to whom. You have to ask the people in that room.

Mr. MICA. Was anyone else in the room?

Mr. RIVOLO. I am confused on that issue because I was under the impression that it was only Admiral Kramek, but my colleague is very certain that there were other people in there, and you will have to ask him. But I suspect that his memory on this issue is much better than mine. I did not make much of——

Mr. MICA. The only one you remember then is Admiral Kramek?

Mr. RIVOLO. Yes, sir.

Mr. MICA. But you think there were others?

Mr. RIVOLO. Yes.

Mr. MICA. After the meeting, did Admiral Kramek emerge and did he apologize to you for the event and also did he indicate in any way that the drug czar had rejected this study or the conclusions?

Mr. RIVOLO. Yes, sir. Admiral Kramek came out. He said, I am sorry, the general does not want to take your briefing at this time; and we were surprised. We asked a question or two, like why; what's wrong?

And basically, he relayed that he does not believe the conclusions and he doesn't like basically the comparison between interdiction and treatment. And, therefore, until further notice, that's the status.

We then drove back——

Mr. MICA. Before you get to that, could I ask you: Did you hear him say or indicate in any way to you that not a word of this is to get out?

Mr. RIVOLO. After the ride back to the Pentagon, where the meeting was going on, the words that were given to us by Admiral Kramek were, well, until further—and there was a long discussion in between. That until further notice, not a word of this can get out, yes, sir.

Mr. MICA. Now, is it your understanding that those were—was that a directive by Admiral Kramek? Or was that something he was passing on from the drug czar?

Mr. RIVOLO. I am not sure it was a directive from anyone. I mean, in principle, no one can stop us except the sponsor, and much of this work was not done for Admiral Kramek. It was done for Mr. Sheridan. However, Admiral Kramek essentially was trying to make the best of the situation, and he said, there is—it was never interpreted as a directive, but we certainly would follow his desires. We have enormous respect for Admiral Kramek.

Mr. MICA. Was it motivated? Do you think Admiral Kramek was the one that was—that wanted—didn't want this information out?

Mr. RIVOLO. No, I do not believe that.

Mr. MICA. So it had to be then—this may be your assumption, but it had to be the drug czar was not pleased with the conclusion that your report reached and took a different position and didn't want that information out; is that—would that be a fair assumption?

Mr. RIVOLO. That would be conjecture on my part, and that is the conjecture that I held at the time.

Mr. MICA. Do you recall anyone telling you that the drug czar physically pushed Admiral Kramek, or the word that I had was that he pushed him against the wall? Did anyone say anything about the conflict that took place in that room?

Mr. RIVOLO. During the ride back, there were some discussions, and I'm not quite sure who was in those discussions, but there were some comments made about the managerial style of General McCaffrey. Everyone knows him. But I would not comment to any substance of anything relating to what went on in the room.

Mr. MICA. Was Mr. Boyer with you, an assistant to Admiral Kramek?

Mr. RIVOLO. That's one of the discrepancies that my colleague and I have in that I was under the impression that he was not. He is under the impression that he was. But I do remember that there were several people in the staff car. Whether the——

Mr. MICA. Do you remember whether it was Admiral Kramek that talked about the severity of the conflict in that discussion or was it someone else?

Mr. RIVOLO. I really don't think Admiral Kramek would comment on things like that. So whatever was said either was by implication or by projection of personalities. I am not quite sure.

Mr. MICA. Did there come a time afterwards when you or one of the other authors contacted someone else in the White House drug czar's office, perhaps maybe a week later, to seek permission to release this report to Members of Congress?

Mr. RIVOLO. It was not—if that happened, that happened through the sponsor's office.

Mr. CRANE. Let me comment.

Mr. MICA. Mr. Crane.

Mr. CRANE. As the project leader.

I sought clarification, after the day when we had the briefings, and I asked the following questions of both sponsors: Do we have any instructions at all to end any of the type of work on price and demand? The answer was absolutely not. In fact, we have produced other briefings. I gave a talk on the 7th and 8th of August using that same data.

So I went to look at, did any of our documents that were published in conference proceedings were they changed with respect to this? I could find no evidence of it. So I have been able to find no evidence of any, you know, taking out or censoring of our material that I am aware of, sir.

Mr. MICA. Mr. Rivolo, again, was there a time shortly after this incident when you or any of the other authors contacted the White House drug czar's office, sought permission to release the report to Members of Congress?

Mr. RIVOLO. Not to my knowledge, and not that I have done. My only time in which that question was asked, it was asked of Admiral Kramek. It was about a week, perhaps, after that event and after we had our usual discussion about typical operations and what was worked and what wasn't. Barry asked the Admiral: "Sir, are we in any way not to discuss any aspect of this?" And he was very adamant about it. He says absolutely not. You guys are doing great work. You continue to do and preach whatever you think is correct. That was the only——

Mr. ZELIFF. The gentleman's time has expired.

Mr. MICA. Thank you, Mr. Chairman.

I will yield back.

Mr. ZELIFF. Dr. Rivolo, how did you feel when, you know, you have been working on this report for how long?

Mr. RIVOLO. About 18 months.

Mr. ZELIFF. Eighteen months. So it's a year and a half and you were probably pretty excited that you had some good information that would be well-received?

Mr. RIVOLO. Yes, sir, because first of all, I did not expect to find what I found, and I thought that the material was very, very timely in light of what was going on inside.

Mr. ZELIFF. Because we were in the process of putting appropriations bills together, working on the new strategy, the new drug czar.

Mr. RIVOLO. I was not so concerned with the appropriations. I was concerned with the strategy in South America in implementing basically the philosophy of PDD–14, where we were going to try to interdict the machinery of cocaine production rather than trying other strategies, and we now had evidence that that strategy would work.

Mr. ZELIFF. How did you feel about not being able to present your report? And how did you feel about the reactions that took place and Admiral Kramek coming back and telling you that it's not going to see the light of day? Just describe your feelings.

Mr. RIVOLO. I was very surprised, but I am very naive in this game. I have been in the academic world too long. I was very surprised and I was angry. I was really angry, because it was not a political statement in any sense.

All it was, here, look at this. We can actually make a connection between what goes on in the interdiction role in South America and the prices on the streets of L.A. and New York. That information needs to be folded in somewhere. It's not my job to do that unless you ask, but this is important information.

Mr. ZELIFF. And if we take a look at what's happened since 1992 in terms of the lack of support for interdiction, it probably says that maybe we are on the wrong path?

Mr. RIVOLO. Uhm——

Mr. ZELIFF. Let me ask you a different question then.

If you see drug use among teenagers soaring, you see that we have an epidemic, you have to go back and take a look at what was working prior to 1992, and take a look at maybe revisiting that and seeing if maybe we have to go back to something that was working; relative to your report, does that commonsense wise say maybe we ought to take another look?

Mr. RIVOLO. I believe that the strategy to fight drugs has to be very broad and incorporate many elements. I believe that the interdiction role, as always, has been dismissed, dismissed by the community at large, and we believe that at this point—I did not believe it 18 months ago—that interdiction has a role and, in fact, can be a very effective role.

The rising trends in young people, I do have my own opinion on that, but whether they are linked or not, I don't know. We do know that in the case of cocaine—and by the way, we have only studied cocaine—that in the case of cocaine, prices hit a record low in late 1994, early 1995.

Mr. ZELIFF. So commonsense wise, the lower the price, the broader the distribution, the more people that will try it?

Mr. RIVOLO. Apparently the law of supply and demand is not heeded to by much of the community. Many people who work in the street do not believe that that law operates. We certainly do.

Mr. ZELIFF. Let me ask you so that I understand; do you believe it operates?

Mr. RIVOLO. Absolutely.

Mr. ZELIFF. OK.

And I guess, Dr. Crane, I looked at this letter from, I guess it was basically from Mr. Boyer, from Admiral Kramek's office to you, Dr. Crane, and relative to changing some of the content of the report, I will just read two paragraphs: "The draft paper on source zone interdiction effectiveness is an excellent step toward quantifying a very complex issue. A linkage between interdiction efforts and cocaine price fluctuations is one that we have intuitively based our supply reduction strategy upon, and it's gratifying to see that the impact can be quantified."

Then in another paragraph: "The discussion of the cost-effectiveness of treatment programs is of great value but not necessary to the analysis of the intrinsic value of the interdiction programs and possibly beyond the purview of USIC or DOD-related taskings for IDA. Recommend this issue be removed from the paper and treated separately or, at a minimum, placed in an appendix so that the interdiction effectiveness discussion can proceed separately." And then a little handwritten note, "good work."

Would you be willing to comment on that?

Mr. CRANE. Yes; we did, in a previous draft, get comments in a previous draft from a different sponsor. However, this is prior to any of these events.

Mr. ZELIFF. Prior to which events?

Mr. CRANE. Well, prior to the May 8 document. And he certainly in no way tried—as you know, it's in the document. He in no way tried to—so I didn't interpret that as any restriction on whether we should put it in or not, and it was one of the many types of letters that we got giving us advice on what to put in the document or not. But I will tell you that we made our own judgment on that. We have very strict rules about independence and no one put us under any pressure and we put in what we felt was appropriate for this draft document.

Mr. ZELIFF. Let me ask Dr. Rivolo, were you asked to soften your approach on treatment?

Mr. RIVOLO. No.

Mr. ZELIFF. Did you leave anything out relative to treatment?

Mr. RIVOLO. And you must realize that my communication and feedback is purely numeric and computer and numbers. Those discussions are handled by Dr. Crane.

Mr. ZELIFF. So you never talked to Mr. Sheridan?

Mr. RIVOLO. We did talk to Mr. Sheridan and his staff many times.

Mr. ZELIFF. And did they suggest you taking treatment out or softening treatment?

Mr. RIVOLO. I never recall any guidance one way or another. Their guidance has always been, you do what you think is best and make sure that it's sound. That's always been the direction.

Mr. ZELIFF. What bothers me is this, the way we do these reports, though, if you do all these drafts and you get all this guidance, what happens to just doing the work? And then we either accept or reject it based on the quality of the report. Why do we have to keep changing it so the people who are doing the report are happy with the results?

Mr. RIVOLO. Unfortunately, some of that goes on. Most of the drafts are really for technical review. People complain about, well, this is not clear, this needs to be amplified, this is incorrect.

Mr. ZELIFF. But did this go on in any of these drafts? Did we alter it so that people would feel better about what they were doing?

Mr. CRANE. Let me comment as the project leader, sir. It's standard procedure to have open discussion with the sponsors and then they express their concerns. They have always given us full freedom to—I shouldn't say full freedom, but a substantial amount of freedom to put in there what we felt was important, and in no way—we always seek that information from them because we might have overlooked something. And they were just one of many.

I would say I did not feel any pressure at all with respect to that. We put in what we felt was appropriate for the draft for the interagency to look at.

Mr. ZELIFF. OK. I guess you said this came out before you started changing the reports, but when Boyer wrote you under Item E: Recommend the leading or softening of any language that appears to be either combative with or condescending of the RAND study, was self-promoting of IDA, instead of taking a negative approach toward the RAND analysis, take a positive approach toward source country efforts and let the IDA analysis speak for itself.

That didn't affect you in any way?

Mr. CRANE. Not that I recall, sir. I mean, we haven't made any changes in the report yet. We are still evaluating all comments.

Mr. ZELIFF. How long does it take to get a report from all the various drafts to a final completion? It has been 18 months and then do we have 6 or 8 months, a couple of years? Then what happens to the effectiveness of the data?

Mr. CRANE. I gave one report to the interagency which involved this material at a classified level and compared it in December. We really didn't begin to write this report until, I would say, February, March, April, and May. It isn't uncommon then, since it had a lot of substance to it, to receive a lot of criticism and try to fix the report and make a better product of it. So we are going through, in my opinion, not only the normal cycle but a faster cycle than I am accustomed to in a lot of our reports.

Mr. COMFORT. Mr. Chairman, if I could just say in that regard, I believe we became aware of our own conclusions in the December time period. We then put them into a briefing form to convey them where we could. We then turned it into a report, a couple of internal drafts, a final draft that you have. We've received a number of comments.

This is ground-breaking work. As a result, we expect it to be somewhat controversial. We are in the process—well along in the process—of reviewing the comments, assessing them and making the changes.

We have been somewhat hampered, I will say, in that some of the comments, some of the constructive comments, were presented to us anonymously. We found from other critiques that we were able to resolve what oftentimes were misunderstandings and miscommunications by sitting down and talking to the people. We have been somewhat hampered and going slower in this because we are not privy to who are the author's of some of the comments.

Mr. ZELIFF. Why do you suppose this is taking place?

Mr. COMFORT. I can only say that we were provided the comments indirectly. Certainly, these reviewers were not anonymous to ONDCP. They were only anonymous when they were presented to us. It is standard practice that academic reviews for journals are conducted by reviewers who are anonymous to the authors. This was never intended, obviously from its tone, to be a paper for an academic journal. So we would welcome a hearty and open discussion with all of those who feel they have valid comments.

Mr. ZELIFF. Meanwhile, as Mr. Cummings says, kids are dying on the streets of Baltimore and other countries around—in other States and countries around the world. It just seems to me that something as vital as a report of this nature, if it's accurate—and again, at some point I guess we are going to have to determine that. After we get through the methodology and all of that, do you think there's general agreement with your final analysis?

Mr. COMFORT. I think that our finding that well-conceived, source-zone operations do have direct effectiveness upon the prices of cocaine in the streets of the United States and upon the purity on the streets, I believe we continue to have strong support for that. I would also——

Mr. ZELIFF. Would that also stand up?

Mr. COMFORT. I believe so.

I would also add the comment you just read from Captain Boyer about his suggestion as to what to do with the RAND analysis and the chart on cost-effectiveness of treatment. We hope in the tone of how we presented the results in that paper, certainly in informal communications which he may have, that we have consistently viewed our work as a work on source-owned interdiction.

While we found these other things, we in no way were attacking the effectiveness of treatment programs. We were merely pointing out, as I mentioned earlier, that the projections of the cost-effectiveness was inconsistent with the actual data that we could gather.

We ourselves, as we indicated in the statement we provided for the record, are concerned that some of the findings we presented were done in a way that allowed easy misinterpretation. So it is not at all an invalid criticism that we make a clear distinction in our report so that people understand what we have studied extensively and feel very comfortable with is the relationship of well-conceived, source-zone operations with the marketplace.

We would not try to suggest that the other things in our paper are at the same level of importance to us or within the objective of our study.

Mr. ZELIFF. So just to finalize this, and then I will turn it over to Mr. Hastert, but from 1992 on, we have done major cuts in source-country programs as well as transit-zone programs. What I am understanding you to say is that based on your research, this is the wrong direction and ought to be revisited?

Mr. COMFORT. We believe, based on our research, that well-conceived, source-zone operations are very effective. That does not mean, as Dr. Crane said in his opening statement, that you can't do foolish things throughout the program or things that aren't as effective as others. We think we have shown through our research the types of operations that can be very cost-effective.

Mr. ZELIFF. Mr. Cummings from Maryland.

Mr. CUMMINGS. Thank you very much.

You all—I think somebody asked you a little earlier, you all understand that you have been sworn here; is that right?

[All witnesses answer in the affirmative.]

Mr. CUMMINGS. And you all know what that means; is that right?

[All witnesses answer in the affirmative.]

Mr. CUMMINGS. I am sure you have an appreciation for one's integrity and reputation; do you not?

And I want to ask you some very, very pointed questions and I want you to be very clear with me. General McCaffrey is a person whom I respect tremendously. And some accusations have been made from this bar, and I want to make sure that we are clear. And as I look down the witness list, you are probably about the only people who can answer the questions.

No. 1, have any of you all felt intimidated with regard to this whole process, this report and getting it out and what have you? Have any of you?

Mr. CRANE. Let me comment that at first we were a little—I think felt a little bit upset that these important findings might not be moving as quickly. Subsequent, when I went and checked for what evidence that any of the reports were suppressed, were we given any guidance not to continue the work, we have continued to use this information with operational forces, as best we can, to improve operations, and given numerous briefings since then. So at first I think we might have felt that way, but today I am not intimidated by it, no, sir.

Mr. CUMMINGS. And to you directly, have you felt any intimidation by General McCaffrey? That's what I am concerned about. This man's reputation is on the line. I am concerned about it.

Mr. CRANE. Sir, I think I just answered that question.

Mr. CUMMINGS. OK, fine.

Mr. COMFORT. Sir, let me say also I have certainly not met the principals in general. As I indicated, I have been the inside author, staying within my office bounds more or less. But as was pointed out by the chairman, I believe the Institute for Defense Analyses has a long history of producing reports where we speak what we think is correct, whether they are proadministration or against policies. Truthfully, in our view, whether it was pro or against or how it would be interpreted, had and has nothing to do with the way we report our research.

Mr. CUMMINGS. Yes, sir.

Mr. RIVOLO. My personal view is that the word intimidation is really not appropriate. There was a day, maybe 2 days, right after that eventful attempt to brief, where I personally felt—if you want to use the word—intimated.

Mr. CUMMINGS. I want you to use a word that is appropriate. We have the press here that are getting ready to write stories, and there has been an accusation that somebody felt intimated, and I want to know the answer, yes or no.

Mr. RIVOLO. We felt that we could not speak freely for that 1 day. Admiral Kramek came back very quickly. We made it—we asked the question very explicitly; are we being told not to do anything? And we were told, absolutely not.

What I would like to point out is that in terms of feeling, and this is long before General McCaffrey came in to that office, is that we felt ignored; that we were not allowed to discuss findings.

But that single event on that 1 day only applied to that particular briefing, which apparently was objectionable.

Mr. CUMMINGS. And I think you used the word "conjecture" at least two or three times during your testimony. And I am just wondering, did you get anything—that whatever feeling you got was that from General McCaffrey? I mean. Is that of something generally from General McCaffrey?

Mr. RIVOLO. No.

Mr. CUMMINGS. All right. Thank you.

Let me ask you another question. Do you know whether—do you all have any direct evidence that General McCaffrey tried to quash this report? That's another accusation that was made. And I think since we are in the public domain we need to be real clear on that with regard to a man's reputation. I mean, we can go straight across. I am just curious.

Mr. RIVOLO. I have no direct evidence.

Mr. CRANE. I have no direct evidence.

Mr. COMFORT. I have never met General McCaffrey and have no evidence of that.

Mr. CUMMINGS. Thank you.

There was one other thing that—there was a phrase used to bury the report. Have you ever felt that you were—General McCaffrey asked you to bury the report?

This is something that came from this bar. And I am just wondering, have any of you felt or do you have any direct evidence that General McCaffrey asked—implied or anything, that you bury the report?

Mr. CRANE. I, myself, have no direct evidence of that.

Mr. RIVOLO. No; the word "bury", I used that word once—in fact, I used it at the meeting—but only referring to the events of the previous 6 months by ONDCP, not by General McCaffrey.

Mr. CUMMINGS. And you, sir?

Mr. COMFORT. I stand by my answer. I have never met General McCaffrey.

Mr. CUMMINGS. Thank you. I just wanted to clear that up.

Let me go on to some other things that I am very interested in. You talked about the whole question of General McCaffrey and the initial—the report that he read. Is that the same report we are talking about today? In other words, the report that he read on the day that this meeting occurred, is that the same report that we are talking about today, the same draft?

Mr. CRANE. Let me comment.

Mr. CUMMINGS. OK.

Mr. CRANE. We had a briefing to give him the material that was classified. At the same time, Admiral Kramek gave him the copy of the report you are discussing. What happened to those things, you would have to ask them.

Mr. CUMMINGS. OK. Now let me make it clear. The document that you gave—I am sorry. I am glad you corrected me. The document that you gave Kramek, first of all, was Kramek aware of all the stuff in the document? Did you brief him?

Mr. CRANE. Yes; we had briefed—there were two—there were two pieces of material. One was a briefing report, secret, on operations. The other was the report that you are referring to in this hearing, and both of those were left with General McCaffrey.

Mr. CUMMINGS. All right. It's this same document, this fourth draft that we are talking about today; is that right?

Mr. CRANE. No, sir. It was probably the third draft or something. I am not sure it's exactly the same.

Mr. CUMMINGS. So you don't know whether the document—you are saying you don't know whether the document that we are dealing with today, this draft, this fourth draft, is the document that was presented that day to General McCaffrey? Am I right?

Mr. CRANE. I think there might have been a change in the preface or two, but it's basically almost identical to the one that you have before you.

Mr. CUMMINGS. Let me ask you this: In talking—I just want you to comment on this. I am just curious. When I talk to the people—I live in a drug-infested area, north of Madison Avenue in Baltimore City. It is drug infested. And I have a chance to talk to a lot of folk that are doing this kind of stuff, and trying to encourage them to get off, get treatment, whatever.

The question—and when I ask them about prices, what they tell me—I just want you to comment if you can. If you can't, that's fine—they tell me that if the price goes up, they just do more crime. I mean, have you ever—I mean, did you all take that into consideration?

In other words, if you have got an addict, the addicts have to have drugs. So the question becomes—I mean, when we talk about effectiveness, I am just curious, did you take that into consideration?

You said you had your own personal opinions and all that kind of stuff. And so I am just wondering about that. I mean, these are the guys—these are the folk who are on the street every day, the ones who break into houses and things, the women who sell their bodies. And I am just wondering, does that have—I mean, did you take any of that into consideration?

Mr. RIVOLO. Yes, we did. And, in fact, we have looked at the uniform crime statistics. We have looked at a huge number of data sources.

Let me just give you a synopsis. When drug prices—when cocaine, and again I address cocaine only, when cocaine prices reversed in 1989 and almost doubled, there was a drop in drug-related homicides, a drop, a significant drop. OK? That has to do with there's less drugs available. There are less dealings going on and the dealers do less shooting. That's one that can be backed up by the Justice Department statistics.

In terms of petty crime, money-raising crime, car thefts, that also shows a drop, although it doesn't appear to be correlated.

However, you can exclude any rise, any rise in those statistics, linked to price rises. Now, again the only major price rise we have ever seen was in 1989 and 1990, and that is the data that we looked at in detail. We are in the process of looking at more current detail, but we have support from the Department of Justice analysts who ought to agree, although I have not seen any reports, that certainly when it comes to drug-related homicides, 1989 was a bucket. It was an all-time low.

Mr. CUMMINGS. Would you agree that the—may I just—chairman, may I just ask one more question?

Mr. ZELIFF. Go ahead.

Mr. CUMMINGS. Thank you. I think you have been kind of lenient with the other side.

Mr. ZELIFF. I have been very lenient with you, my friend.

Mr. CUMMINGS. Let me ask you this: When you look at—homicides are very significant, don't get me wrong. But it is the petty crimes, it is the breaking into houses, breaking into cars, taking car phones and things of that nature, sell them for $50 and whatever, I mean, that's very—I mean, homicides are significant. But I think the petty—when you are trying to get money to buy some crack cocaine and get it quickly, it seems like that would have more relevance than, say, the murders.

Mr. RIVOLO. I know that is the accepted paradigm. We see no evidence for it. And we also might point to previous research done in the 1970's relating crime to heroin use which came to the same conclusions.

Mr. CUMMINGS. Thank you.

Mr. ZELIFF. The gentleman's time has expired.

Mr. Hastert.

Mr. HASTERT. I thank the chairman.

First, I want to get this clear, because I am completely amazed from my friend from the other side of the aisle saying that through his anecdotal research on the streets of Baltimore that he would think that if you make great amounts of narcotics available you will reduce the amount of crime. I am not sure how you figure that, but if that's the point that he is trying to make, I really have a hard time understanding that.

But I want to ask you—because you haven't done anecdotal research. You have done real research. You have set up cause-and-effect type of situations. As a physicist, you can do that, I guess, best.

I have to make some—I have always said that I have been appropriately apologetic for saying that I am an economist. I always remember one of my good friends who grew up with me in the cornfields of Illinois. He wanted to be an economist, but as a youth he had his hand taken off by a cornpicker. The story was he could never get accepted into the school of economics because most economic sayings are, well, on the other hand, and he just didn't qualify.

So I understand the softness of economic theory and the models. I have been involved in putting economic models together. And they are just that, economic models. And there is—sometimes relation to reality, there's not a lot there.

But in your study, you went through and tried to show a correlation, that if you can stop the amount of drugs flowing through the pipeline, through huge events such as the shoot-down policy in

Peru or the shutting down of a huge drug lab in Colombia, that there was actually a difference, there was an increase in price on the streets and, as you said, according to my friend from Maryland's question, that there was actually a decrease in crime.

Now, we spend $90 billion a year, $90 billion a year, not on interdiction, not on this, but from the crime aspect, victims of crime, prosecuting criminals, all tied into drugs and those deaths of teenagers. The same teenagers that are on the streets of Baltimore who get this stuff sometimes because the price is cheap and they can afford to get it for a recreational drug, where they would never have been able to buy it as a recreational drug prior if the price was so high that they couldn't afford it. It was before they get hooked on this substance, before they go out committing crimes because they have to have it.

Now, let me ask you a question. Is it relevant that if there's some type of study that shows that you can squeeze down the pipeline of drugs coming into this country and it makes a difference in the price of narcotics, cocaine in this situation, the purity of cocaine in this situation and the incidents of crime in this situation, and it flies in the face of the so-called RAND study, that the administration has adhered to since 1993, that basically shows twice the number of drug use in this country since that period of time, that shows our teenagers have gotten into marijuana and other drugs sometimes up to a 400 percent increase between certain age groups, that's a pretty relevant thing, is it not?

Mr. RIVOLO. It's extremely relevant if you believe those connections. Many of our colleagues in the economics community and the social scientists do not believe it. They dismiss all of these points of attachment, which we believe are now black and white.

Mr. HASTERT. Let me come out of the world of social science because I taught social science for a lot of years, more years than I want to talk about. But social science, many people in the world of social science will say, here is a problem, let's do a study to show why this problem exists. They don't usually use a lot of empirical evidence. They are not physicists like in your situation.

Now, let's say here is what has happened since 1992: That this administration has taken in—before General McCaffrey. I have to tell my friend from Maryland, I have a great deal of respect for General McCaffrey who came out as a four-star general, commanded the southern command, knows about drug interdiction. But even before he became the drug czar, there was $500 million that was taken out of interdiction. There was $200 million that came out of the ability for us to be able to even interdict, go out and have the Coast Guard planes and the trains——

Mr. ZELIFF. Will the gentleman yield for just a second?

Mr. HASTERT. Yes.

Mr. ZELIFF. How about just drastically cutting and gutting the drug czar's office so that whoever the drug czar is doesn't have the resources to do the work?

Mr. HASTERT. One of the things that I find somewhat repulsive, and I think the gentleman from Maryland will probably agree with me, is that when the White House said, well, we cut White House staff, they did. They cut everybody in the drug office. So that was how we could cut White House staff.

But let me make an important point before my time is up. That the Coast Guard had $400 million taken out of its budget. These are the people who were successful before 1993 in stopping narcotic air traffic and narcotic traffic coming through boats, through our Mediterranean—Caribbean and in some cases, the Western, Near Western Pacific—I am sorry Eastern Pacific, which is along our Western coast and Mexico's Western coast.

We had $300 million from 1993 to 1996 taken out of source-country interdiction, the very thing that I was saying that shows some real correlations between the study you did and the study—and the results of what happens on the street. And $1 billion of that money, that savings, went into treatment.

Now, I don't think there is anything wrong with treatment, but I think you are putting the cart before the horse, quite frankly, when you say we have to put $1 billion more in treatment, we are going to take it out of drug interdiction and source-country actions because we have lowered the price of drugs on the street and we have got a lot more kids being hooked on drugs because of the low prices and increased purity. Because of the drug actions that we have had in this country over the last 4 years that we have to put another billion dollars in interdiction—or in drug treatment, because we have a lot more kids hooked, I think really is a—turning the world upside down or putting logic on its head, if you will.

What we have tried to do is take some of that money and put at least $200 million more into the drug interdiction of the Coast Guard. We have tried to give some of this money into General McCaffrey. We have given him $60 million to use at his discretion. We want to know how he is going to use it but—so that he can do a better job.

So the signs that you have created and the study that you have created that shows that there's a correlation between shutting down drug interdiction in foreign source countries, Bolivia, Peru, Colombia, and what happens on the street, is pretty relevant, especially because if we have to spend an extra billion dollars in treatment because of those kids that got hooked on the street because you took that drug interdiction money away.

And when I go to the chairman, subcommittee chairman, on Transportation and say we have to help the Coast Guard stop this drug stuff, we have to squeeze down the pipeline, and he waves the RAND study in my face, then we need to be able to counter that study. And that's exactly what we have done. And if we play ignorance and say, well, we can't do this because we don't see it, then there's something wrong in the system.

I can tell you, you can have all kinds of models to put in the RAND study, but the RAND study doesn't wash as far as I am concerned. And the cause and effect that you have put together does wash. There's relevance and some kind of a correlation between facts—factual information. That's what we want to see.

And, you know, I don't know. There's figurative language and there's literal language and as you—again, my good friend from Maryland has said—somebody said in that car on the way to the Pentagon, that General McCaffrey put somebody up against the wall, that's military language. I know that. It could be literally against the wall. It could be figuratively up against the wall.

And as a new drug czar, he may have reason to try to get his feet on the ground and try to find out what's fact and what's fiction. But in the long run, we need to be able to give the American people the right information. We need to have Congress and all of those people out there who are fighting that drug war to have the right information so they can do the right things.

I think your study, in my opinion, as an economist who sometimes makes mistakes—it goes a long way toward that. I yield back.

Mr. ZELIFF. Gentleman from Florida, Mr. Mica.

Mr. MICA. Thank you, Mr. Chairman.

Mr. Rivolo, did you write a memo to certain individuals explaining the White House mindset or the drug czar mindset against the release of the report?

Mr. RIVOLO. I wrote a memo to my boss at IDA, who appended it to his own version, the memo that essentially came to the defense of the criticism that came from ONDCP, and the memo essentially said the work is sound, it needs to be debated in open community, not by the experts of ONDCP, and the consequences of this are important enough that you need to open up the machinery, and I was very critical in my language.

Mr. MICA. Did you provide that memo to Deputy Assistant Secretary of State Brian Sheridan?

Mr. RIVOLO. The memo was delivered to Mr. Sheridan, that is correct.

Mr. MICA. Do you have a copy of that memo? I have asked for a copy of that memo, and I haven't gotten a copy of the memo.

Mr. RIVOLO. I had a copy of the memo that actually went to Mr. Newberry, who was in that office.

Mr. MICA. Would you provide a copy of that memo to the committee?

Mr. RIVOLO. I certainly can. But that memo to Mr. Newberry behind it is a memo from me to Mr. Tom Christie, my direct supervisor.

Mr. MICA. When you read the memo from Barry Crane to Brian Sheridan to Tom Christie seeking to get this report released and disseminated given the urgency of the Nation's drug problem, did there come a time when you thought you should reveal this information?

Mr. RIVOLO. Reveal to whom?

Mr. MICA. Well, to anyone.

Mr. RIVOLO. I believe that the information should have been made public, yes. And I pushed that point of view very strongly to Mr. Sheridan and his staff.

Mr. MICA. Well, do you also recall a memo written from within the administration back in 1994–95 which was a direct indictment of the RAND study promoting treatment, which was a study commissioned by the White House? Do you by chance have a copy of that internal critique of the RAND study with you?

Mr. RIVOLO. That was not a memo. It was a draft paper which was done at the request of Mr. Sheridan. It was written by me, delivered to Mr. Sheridan not in a memo form, but as a draft document. I have a computer version of that. It is all I can find.

Mr. MICA. Could you provide a copy of that?

Mr. RIVOLO. I certainly can.

Mr. MICA. Are you aware that Congress has never received those documents from Sheridan, McCaffrey, Kramek, or any other office from whom we have requested them?

Mr. RIVOLO. No, I was not aware.

Mr. MICA. Let me ask you. Were you ever involved in a conversation with Barry Crane, and did he ever say to you that he was afraid that someone was trying to bury this report?

Mr. RIVOLO. Shortly after the events of the briefing, which was, as I said, lasted for about 2 days, Dr. Crane was upset and essentially made the remark that this is the absolute wrong thing to do because it will look like a coverup.

Mr. MICA. Dr. Crane, is that what you said?

Mr. CRANE. I don't recall exactly that language.

Mr. MICA. Did you say, someone is trying to bury this report?

Mr. CRANE. I don't recall that language. Let me say, though, I was upset at that time. What I did was immediately seek clarification, see if there was any evidence——

Mr. MICA. Mr. Comfort, were you aware of any of this conversation?

Mr. COMFORT. Again, as I say, I wasn't there. I would say that when both of these briefers came back, they certainly were upset at the time. I think they felt they had done good work. I believe we had done good work. I would not at all be surprised, though I do not recall any of that language, that that was their feeling at the time.

Mr. MICA. Did you hear anyone say that McCaffrey had told Kramek that: "not a word of this is to get out"?

Mr. COMFORT. Again, I could not recall any specific language at the time, but I believe that kind of feeling, which clearly was conjecture since none of us were in the room, might well have been spoken and might have expressed their feelings at the time.

Mr. MICA. You never heard that comment?

Mr. COMFORT. I can't recall that I ever heard those specific words. I will say, as Dr. Rivolo just mentioned, that I have heard Dr. Crane in just standing around the coffee pot, so to speak, suggest that he thought it was a mistake that our paper not be given more open discussion because he was concerned that it would look like somebody was trying to bury our paper.

Mr. MICA. So that was the comment that you made?

Mr. COMFORT. I recall that sort of conversation.

Mr. MICA. Mr. Rivolo, General McCaffrey testified before me when I asked him about this before that your report was: "utter nonsense," contained utter nonsense. Did you brief the General prior to—at any time prior to the March meeting that you went to?

Mr. RIVOLO. No, sir.

Mr. MICA. Are you aware that the general had a copy of the—did he have a copy of the report?

Mr. RIVOLO. He had a copy of the report and the annotated briefing, yes, sir.

Mr. MICA. When was that given to him?

Mr. RIVOLO. The day of the interagency meeting, which I believe was May 7.

Mr. CRANE. May 8.

Mr. RIVOLO. May 8.

Mr. MICA. I am talking about in March, he told me when he got the report, he thought it was utter nonsense.

Mr. CRANE. We didn't give anything to him until May 8.

Mr. MICA. Is there anything in the report either in the March or May version that is utter nonsense?

Mr. RIVOLO. No, sir.

Mr. MICA. Is there anything in this report in the March version—and I don't have a copy of it, but we will get it—or the May version that is utter nonsense?

Mr. CRANE. In my opinion, no.

Mr. MICA. Dr. Comfort, is there anything in this report in any version, March, May, June, July, any copy that hasn't been released, that is utter nonsense, that you would term utter nonsense?

Mr. COMFORT. There is one figure that is subject to misinterpretation, but there is nothing that is utter nonsense.

Mr. MICA. Thank you.

I yield back.

Mr. ZELIFF. The gentleman from Pennsylvania.

Mr. Clinger.

Mr. CLINGER. Thank you very much, Mr. Chairman.

Gentlemen, we thank you for your testimony here today.

I think that, as I represent a district that has probably more Federal prisons than any other district in the country, Lewisburg, Bradford, and Oliver, and as I meet with the wardens of those prisons, the thing that comes through loud and clear is that the major crime problem in this country is the drug problem; that 80 to 90 percent of the prisoners that were incarcerated now are there because of either direct or indirect drug connections, crimes committed because of drugs, crimes committed with drugs directly. It is enormous.

I think we tend to underestimate the social cost of this problem, and therefore that is why it becomes so absolutely critical that we don't waste resources, that we use the resources in a wise and sensible and effective way to address the problem.

The graph would suggest that we are losing the war, that we are, in fact, going backward. It becomes all the more imperative and urgent that we have clear, precise, accurate information on which to base judgments. That is our job up here, our job in this committee.

The job of the Government Reform and Oversight Committee is to conduct oversight. That is an exercise that is often scoffed at, an exercise that is perceived as political witch-hunting, as something that you have to put up with in the legislative process, but it is really just window dressing. I know no member of this committee who views our role as just window dressing. We really view it as something of vital importance, and I think nothing could emphasize that more than the nature of this problem.

The reason we are here today, we feel very strongly that in order to make sensible decisions and recommendations to our colleagues on the results of oversight and what that oversight has produced, we have to have accurate information. If we don't have all of the information, then that judgment and that recommendation is going to be flawed, and in this case we clearly didn't have all the information at a time when it would have been very helpful to have that information, when we are really talking about where we put our money. Where do we put the bucks? Where are they going to be most effectively used? The policy has been to put that emphasis on remediation and to put it on treatment, and rather than on interdiction, on what appears to be flawed grounds that that was a failed policy, that interdiction was not working. So, I guess the concern we have is that we need to have that information.

Now we have seen too often here that this—that is why we need to get to the bottom of, was this suppressed, was this deliberately suppressed, was there a conscious effort to withhold this information, because it would undercut a policy, or was there some other reason why it was withheld? Maybe it is flawed. You gentlemen stand behind it. You said there is certainly no nonsense to this report; that is, it is scientifically strong, and you can back it up. So, in that case we do have conflicting views as to where we ought to be going with this thing. We can't make a judgment unless we have both those views before us. We did not have your view, we did not have your studied scientific objective, we believe, in consideration of this whole problem.

So, we have all—most recently we now have a claim of executive privilege over documents that might be helpful to us in making that assessment. I believe, Mr. Chairman, we had a memo from—this was a letter to Mr. Quinn—or to Chairman Zeliff from Mr. Quinn in which he claims executive privilege over a document that might be very helpful to our examination.

So, I guess my question to you—a couple of questions, No. 1, some confusion over what the status of this report is. We had a March version, a May version, various other versions. Did you consider this work product a final report?

Dr. Crane.

Mr. CRANE. What I would like to do is go through the sequence of how we produce a substantive report. At the stage of May 8, we were going to have some comment from interagency. We were releasing it from the inside route. That process went on—it went into Government hands, and we know that the distribution was made. What we would do is get these comments back—I have a very substantial comment file. We got the comments back, and we are addressing the criticisms.

Now those criticisms are very, very valuable to scientists because they improve not only our ability to make our case, but they also expose any weakness in our logic. Because this became quite a controversial issue, on August 30, I received a list of distinguished people from the National Research Council so that we could provide them to do much higher level review of not only our own documents, but also the ones that we have differences in findings. So it is our intention to go through the formal review process to make a report, and we are just going along in that process. And what's happened here is we stumbled into the middle of the scientific debate.

Mr. CLINGER. Let me interrupt you here. Just to reference a memo that you did send to Brian Sheridan in July in which you said that the failure to disseminate and use these new research results—which I assume is what we are talking about here—optimally and employing and motivating the limited allied forces may put in jeopardy future source-zone performance against cocaine production. So, you felt in July that this was a matter of some urgency.

Mr. CRANE. Let me say, to put in context, this report is 1 of maybe 20 things we work on. My principal support to Admiral Kramek and Brian Sheridan is to provide operational advice. This report—I didn't mention the word "report" in there at all other than there were some criticisms of it. There is an ongoing operation, sir, right now that I needed to put certain types of this information. I wanted to be absolutely sure. It had to get out, and, in fact, all the recommendations in it have been complied with. We have briefed the people at the conference in August, so I am satisfied that that has happened.

Mr. CLINGER. I have just one further question, Mr. Chairman, if I may.

Dr. Rivolo, you answered earlier, and I was not here when you did answer, Congressman Cummings' question that you didn't have any direct evidence that General McCaffrey was directing this report be quashed. However, I think you intimated that the ONDCP staff may have tried to influence this report in some way; that you felt you had some intimations or suggestions that there may have been staff influence. Could you elaborate? Do you have any specifics?

Mr. RIVOLO. Yes; as I said, there were many, many months before General McCaffrey actually took that office. We had findings, and we were briefing the interagencies as early as March 1995, that there was some significant connection between the interdiction events and what was happening in the streets. We felt this was important and new because it contradicted the standard view of things, and we tried to bring that into ONDCP, and we tried many times. We had Mr. Sheridan attempt. We had his staff attempt. We also, for many months, requested data, Department of Justice data, Health and Human Services data, and all of that had to be approved through ONDCP. Those things didn't happen. They happened extremely slowly or did not happen at all.

This was our view—I should say my view, I, maybe my colleague, because I was working very closely with the people that handled the data—that office was not interested in listening to what we had to say. That was my perception, and I hold it to this day.

Mr. CLINGER. It went beyond just bureaucratic lethargy or the bureaucratic slowdowns; it went beyond that?

Mr. RIVOLO. Yes; that is my perception.

Mr. CLINGER. Thank you.

Mr. ZELIFF. I just had a quick question here. You all referred to a secret report, a briefing, that was apparently given to certain members of the administration as an addendum to one of the reports that we have here; is that correct? We were wondering if we could get a copy of that secret report.

Mr. CRANE. Could you give us the date? You mean the day of this report; is that what you are referring to?

Mr. ZELIFF. I believe, Dr. Crane, you referred to the secret report. It is something you have and we don't have, and if you could give me the date, that is the one we want.

Mr. CRANE. There was a secret report, the briefing materials that we had, and we could provide that to you, sir.

Mr. ZELIFF. Thank you, sir.

I guess the only last comment I would make is that the report you all are working on took 18 months. It was presented initially in March. It is now March, April, May, June, July, August; we are in September, October. You know, it wasn't buried, it wasn't delayed, it wasn't suppressed. I don't know; what was it? When does it get done, and at what point does it have any relevant value? Again, General McCaffrey came in here and got sworn in in February, and I attended that swearing-in ceremony, so we are not criticizing him. We are criticizing bad data that he will basically then use to come up with 1996 programs, 1997 appropriations. So when, in the year 2000, when will this thing be done? And admittedly it wasn't buried or delayed.

Mr. CRANE. I want to again put into context that we do a lot of work. We have limitations in accelerating that work. As you know, the FFRDC's are restricted from—I can't hire more people because of ceilings on us and so on.

To be fair, we have made many reports at the secret level about this material to the interagency, and that is the proper forum. You will see as you go back, this is just one little piece of it. The principal communication that we make is to the forces, assessments of how they perform, and we use this material where we could to improve their performance, and those, I think, are all a matter for the record and exist.

Mr. ZELIFF. Dr. Crane, you don't feel it has been delayed?

Mr. CRANE. Now that I have a chance to look back on all of the questions to make our case, I feel it certainly is appropriate that we take a lot of caution. We——

Mr. ZELIFF. You don't feel it's been delayed? This is normal?

Mr. CRANE. If we answer the things correctly, I don't feel that report—it is only one of three or four.

Mr. COMFORT. Sir, having seen a lot of documents go forward, certainly in our view when we sent forward a final draft document, the document makes very clear on the inside cover that we issue it as a document because it is preliminary and tentative analysis—we felt at that time that that document was ready for open discussion in the scientific community. We believe that since that time, in working as best as we could to respond to valuable criticisms, we are close to getting all of those understood and responded to. It has been going slower than any of us would like it to happen.

Mr. ZELIFF. Dr. Rivolo.

Mr. RIVOLO. I believe that any time a document comes out of IDA and is controversial, it does take a long time.

Mr. ZELIFF. Seven months on top of 18 is not a big deal?

Mr. RIVOLO. I think the document is irrelevant. I think the information should have been disseminated for open discussion way before that; yes.

Mr. ZELIFF. So can I use the word "delayed"? What would you use? I haven't been around——

Mr. RIVOLO. In a normal environment, the promulgation of information is immediate. Someone says something. It is put on the table and debated. If it is junk, it is very quickly shown to be junk. If it is substantial, it is very quickly shown to be so.

Mr. ZELIFF. What word would you use?

Mr. RIVOLO. My word would be that the document itself is probably on course. That is a controversial document. It is not being delayed. The information has clearly been delayed.

Mr. ZELIFF. Information in a document has been delayed, but the document itself is on course. That is good enough for Government work.

Let me just ask you one comment, Dr. Crane. In your memo of July—and I just refer to you, these findings—once again on page 3 down at the bottom—deserve attention at the highest levels. The failure to advocate and support these findings potentially jeopardize future effectiveness.

Mr. CRANE. Yes, sir; let me comment on that. As everyone who knows me, and at the beginning of the air bridge operations, I certainly made similar-type arguments at the critical times of operations. And we have another operation, which I don't want to get into at the hearing here, but this is a critical operational time, and I will tell you that after giving that document to Mr. Sheridan and Admiral Kramek, that within a week or two action was taken, and I did get a chance in an open session to brief the deputy director of supply reduction at the interagency, and we went over a lot of this information. So from my point of view, it achieved its purpose as to advise Admiral Kramek to act, and, in fact, that happened.

Mr. ZELIFF. But the oversight committee doesn't have a right to participate in this process?

Mr. CRANE. Sir, I do not work for the oversight committee, and you have to speak with Admiral Kramek about what information he makes available to you.

Mr. ZELIFF. We will ask that later.

Mr. Cummings.

Mr. CUMMINGS. Mr. Chairman, I assume we are finished with this round; is that it?

Very well. Let me ask you—yes, I do have questions. Tell me something. It is my understanding that DOD sends your draft report to the National Research Council for review. Has the National Research Council reviewed your draft, and if so, can you provide the subcommittee with a copy of that review?

Mr. CRANE. Let me comment on that. We are going through the process to do that. I received a list of potential reviewers. They took a brief look at it. We do not have any review from the NRC in our hand. That is something that we will do as part of making a paper out of it, an outside independent authority, and we are just setting up that process now.

Mr. CUMMINGS. How long do you think that will take? The chairman, and rightfully so, is very concerned about this report getting out, and I think everyone here shared that we want to see the final report. When do you think all that will be complete? Is that the last stage? Is there still more after that?

Mr. CRANE. No, I think we have a lot of comments to put in there and clarifications, and we will certainly do that where there is confusion.

Just giving a ballpark figure, I think in the next few months we will have to go back and take a look at what manpower is available and ongoing operations, and obviously there is a lot more priority on this document than a week ago, so I will have to give that some more thought.

Mr. CUMMINGS. A week ago it was not that much of a priority.

Mr. CRANE. I think there was some priority, but clearly we are making information available—when this all broke loose, I was in Panama. So that was my first priority, and to be honest with you, I think to get this out I will certainly increase the priority in this area.

Mr. COMFORT. Mr. Cummings, I would like to point out that the distribution of our draft reports belongs to our sponsors. We have no problems with that draft final report being distributed if our sponsor chooses to do that. We can crank out another report that we believe is final quite rapidly.

We have pretty much gone through the forms as we understand them. Because of all of the publicity this has received in the past few weeks, and because we know there is—it's new work, it is pioneering work, and it has received a lot of criticism, we think a review by something like the National Research Council might be worthwhile. If our sponsor wants to conduct that, and if he wants us on our own to conduct that, we can certainly do that. But we would, on our own, certainly not tell you that we can't get the report out before another 2 or 3 months.

Mr. CUMMINGS. So, therefore, we will probably have a report within——

Mr. COMFORT. I would feel comfortable that we could have a report out to our sponsor in the next 3 to 4 weeks. How our sponsors want to distribute that——

Mr. CUMMINGS. What do you think of the peer review comments obtained by ONDCP? I am just curious, what did you think of them?

Mr. CRANE. I will first comment, I think, because this is new work, this type of thing is not uncommon in my past experience to have a lot of debates. We have a lot of data they have not seen. They saw only 1 graph out of 10,000. We have a tremendous amount of data. We really need to sit down and have an open forum on this. But we have a lot of data we can put in there and support our position.

I think it comes down to, from my understanding, a view of how the system works versus the conventional view, and the data we have, we just can't make the two match up. The data says it is working a different way, and we are physical scientists, and we have to go with the data. We may know our prior assumptions about how there was a retail wholesale market and know prior assumptions about what type of model we first use and what we have been reporting really is the raw data, not even a model result yet.

Mr. COMFORT. I would also say, Mr. Cummings, it is clear to us in hindsight that we, in several cases, were unsophisticated in our choice of some terms that are well defined in the economics community. We used them to mean similar but not exactly the same things, and we were taken severely to task for that.

Mr. CUMMINGS. Somebody said that back there, when this report was initially presented to Mr. McCaffrey, that you all thought some other people were in the room. Who said that? I don't remember.

Mr. RIVOLO. I said that.

Mr. CUMMINGS. Who do you think was in the room? I am just curious. We may want to bring them up for questioning.

Mr. RIVOLO. The person is Captain Boyer, if, in fact, he was there. I was not sure, but conversation with my colleagues seems to indicate that Captain Boyer may have been present in that meeting.

Mr. CUMMINGS. Can any of you explain if your pre-1990, 1989 data were adjusted to take into account interdiction policies prior to 1989?

Mr. CRANE. We have since looked at that data. That was actually a valuable criticism, and we were able to measure certain things about operations that DEA ran against the Tranquilandia Complex. We have taken care of that since we received criticism in that area.

Mr. CUMMINGS. I am running out of time. I want to thank all for sharing this information. I certainly look forward to reading the final draft.

I think we are all concerned about what we are trying to address here, and that is drug addiction and deaths and crime that come from it. I wanted to take a moment to thank you all, and I really appreciate your candor.

Mr. ZELIFF. Thank you, Mr. Cummings.

Mr. Hastert.

Mr. HASTERT. Let me just clarify one of the questions my good friend from Maryland asked. Prior to 1989, 1986, 1987, cocaine was really just coming on the scene, wasn't it; wasn't that something relatively new replacing heroin?

Mr. RIVOLO. No, sir. The cocaine epidemic peaked around 1986. Demand has been declining ever since.

Mr. HASTERT. Let me ask you a question. Before you got here and you knew you were going to come, Mr. Rivolo, are you aware that meetings or conversations occurred throughout the past weekend and even yesterday among those who testified today; are you aware of those?

Mr. RIVOLO. No, sir.

Mr. HASTERT. There were no meetings or anything that people wanted to talk together and make sure that they got?

Mr. RIVOLO. You mean within the company?

Mr. HASTERT. Yes.

Mr. RIVOLO. There were meetings between the three of us.

Mr. HASTERT. Anybody else?

Mr. RIVOLO. We also had a short meeting with the president—president of the company, that is.

Mr. HASTERT. I would say that would be interesting.

So you know of no other meetings that took place this weekend?

Mr. RIVOLO. No, sir. In fact, I was away on unrelated business having to do with radars. I just came back on Sunday.

Mr. HASTERT. Thank you.

Let me also ask Mr. Crane. One of the questions here from my friend from the other side of the aisle is that you never actually

45-081 98 - 3

briefed General McCaffrey. You said, no, you never did talk to General McCaffrey, and as a matter of fact, you said you never met General McCaffrey. Part of the reason is that you didn't brief him on the data that you went to brief him; is that correct?

Mr. CRANE. Dr. Comfort didn't—just Dr. Rivolo and I attended the meetings that day. Dr. Comfort did not attend.

Mr. HASTERT. But you attended the meeting, but you never were there to finish the purpose for which it went; is that correct? That was to brief General McCaffrey.

Mr. CRANE. The way it went that day——

Mr. HASTERT. I am asking, you went to brief him that day, Admiral Kramek went in before you, took some of your information, came out and said the briefing would not be necessary. Is that basically it?

Mr. CRANE. The words I recall is that he did not take the briefing, which a standard thing that he wasn't going to accept the briefing from us, that is the way I took it.

Mr. HASTERT. You never did have a chance to brief him, so people could ask questions like we ask today actually never took place?

Mr. CRANE. That is correct.

Mr. HASTERT. Dr. Crane, is that correct?

Mr. CRANE. That is correct.

Mr. HASTERT. I am going to go back and ask here—there was a draft paper on source-zone interdiction effectiveness, and is called an excellent step toward quantifying a very complex issue. One of the things it had, the empirical examination of counter-drug-interdiction program effectiveness. That was what is in your report, was it not, the original draft?

Mr. CRANE. I am not sure if I understand what your question was, sir.

Mr. HASTERT. The information on the source-zone interdiction effectiveness was in your original draft, was it not, one of your original drafts, Dr. Comfort?

Mr. COMFORT. Yes, all of our drafts of this paper have always contained the same basic information on source-zone effectiveness.

Mr. HASTERT. Was there or was there not a recommendation to limiting or softening any language that appears to be either combative or condescending to the RAND study or self-promoting of the IDA study instead of taking a negative approach toward the RAND analysis? Do you know if there was any suggestion to soften that language or change that language?

Mr. CRANE. There were clearly recommendations where we might have used phraseology in a previous study, and people make recommendations to us. I don't believe we softened any of our findings. We might have done a better job.

Mr. HASTERT. Where did that recommendation come from; do you recall?

Mr. CRANE. As I recall the USIC might have made that recommendation, but I don't have the paper, but his staff—however, again, you can clearly see we didn't change any of our conclusions or anything like that.

Mr. HASTERT. Mr. Rivolo, do you recall any pressure to change any language?

Mr. RIVOLO. No. The suggestion—let me relay events. When I was asked to do the initial analysis of the RAND report, the first RAND report, which was modeling the demand for cocaine, which feeds the second report, which is the one that is always being discussed, when I made that analysis, I wrote up a very technical detail of who did what and what was done wrong and what was done right. That document was then turned over internally specifically to Dr. Comfort, who ultimately wrote most of the document. He acted as the redactor, as that word is used, and in the process it was his feeling that my technical critique was much too critical for open discussion. I agreed with it because that was never meant to be a stand-alone document. The draft of that document was never meant to go through the IDA process. It went directly to Mr. Sheridan's office. That document was then incorporated in large part in an appendix of the document that we are now discussing. And the discussion about the terms and the language was strictly internal, mostly from Dr. Comfort.

Mr. HASTERT. Basically there were nine pages on the flaws and treatment of the RAND study in your study, and somebody asked to get it out; is that right, or is that wrong?

Mr. RIVOLO. My—I don't know. The answer is that what I did was analyze the first paper, which did nothing addressing the effectiveness of treatment. First paper is strictly modeling the demand for cocaine. My analysis says there is a serious problem here. When the actual document was written to incorporate the second document of which Dr. Comfort did most of the work, there may have been some discussion, and we were discussing it last night or this morning, that perhaps at some point someone said, maybe you shouldn't be so critical of that.

Mr. HASTERT. Someone might have been?

Mr. CRANE. As the project leader, I made the following decisions. I thought just putting out a very detailed critique of somebody else's work is probably not the best thing. What we waited for before we published the report is we had hard data from events that we—I don't want to say prediction here, but we pretty well analyzed that it was going to happen. It was much more important to make our case from hard data. I made the decision myself not to put out just a detailed critique because I didn't think that was appropriate.

Mr. HASTERT. Let me ask this one final question—my time is running out—to all three of you. In your report, or draft, or final draft, or anything that hasn't been made public—and it does really reflect on future policy of what we do in this country toward how we treat the drug problem that we have—did you—do you stand by the information and the cause-and-effect information that you have published in this draft, or you put out in this draft. The fact is that you can choke down in some type of a major event either in the transportation pipeline for drugs or do away with major production of those drugs in countries like Peru and Colombia, that you can affect the cost of drugs in the market and the purity of drugs in the market?

Mr. CRANE. Absolutely.

Mr. HASTERT. Thank you. I yield back.

Mr. ZELIFF. Mr. Mica.

Mr. MICA. Thank you.

Dr. Crane, did you or Rex Rivolo receive a memo from Admiral Kramek's top assistant Gary Boyer in April of this year before the May, quote, final draft was completed stating that you should remove the conclusions in your report that were critical of the administration's heavy emphasis on drug treatment's effectiveness; specifically that you should remove your criticism of the administration commission of the RAND study that promoted treatment?

Mr. CRANE. I received a memo, we had discussed about it, and we didn't obviously remove that material.

Mr. COMFORT. Can I just comment. As Dr. Rivolo said, I served as redactor for this final draft. I believe I was the person deciding primarily how to say it—what words to put in. If such a memo existed, I was not aware of it. I certainly had my own concerns as to how much emphasis we place on the RAND report because we didn't want our primary findings confused with our secondary findings, but I felt no pressure.

Mr. MICA. Dr. Crane, are you aware of the existence of such a memo?

Mr. CRANE. I recall a memo from Admiral Kramek's office giving some suggestive guidance.

Mr. MICA. Do you have a copy of that memo?

Mr. CRANE. I do not at this time have a copy of it.

Mr. MICA. Dr. Rivolo, are you aware of that memo?

Mr. RIVOLO. Only through discussions with my colleagues. I have never seen the memo.

Mr. MICA. I have a copy now which you provided me of this July response to the drug czar's comments on your draft to Robert Newberry, Office of Secretary of Defense. In this—in your defense, while they are trying to study this report to death here, I want to read from page 3. It says, "although it is true that many of the data bases are very convoluted and contain many sources of possible confounding information, we have developed empirical evidence, not modeled results, for negative correlation between price and demand, measured both by prevalence and consumption in no fewer than six totally independent data sets. These indicators include, one"—and these are six different—"the Drug Abuse Warning Network, DAWN,"—which we are all familiar with—"the Drug Usage Forecast data base; the treatment episode data base; the SmithKline Beacham Clinical Laboratories drug testing data base; the Uniform Crime Reporting data base, the National Household Survey on Drug Abuse data base."

Would you say—and I am not a rocket scientist—I am not a scientist, but what would you say, Dr. Rivolo, this is pretty good confirmation of your conclusions?

Mr. RIVOLO. Yes, sir. In fact, when we first saw the first inkling which came out of the DAWN data, the severe criticism that it was a coincidence; the correlation was there, but it was just a coincidence.

Mr. MICA. I see in the concluding remarks that were prepared that you suggest that, first, the long-sought interchange meeting with the drug czar's office scientist be made to happen. Was there a delay in those meetings?

Mr. RIVOLO. As I have alluded to before, that for many months prior to the new czar taking his position, that we had made many, many, attempts——

Mr. MICA. Repeated attempts that an open—this is another recommendation—that an open conference on the issues be sponsored jointly by the DOD and the drug czar's office to be held in the very near future. Was that done?

Mr. RIVOLO. No, sir.

Mr. MICA. This is in July.

Third, that unbiased, competent authority such as the National Research Council be jointly recruited to shed light on issues. Was that done?

Mr. RIVOLO. No, sir.

Mr. CRANE. We are in the process of doing that, to be fair. I do have a list of NRC people.

Mr. MICA. That will come out in November/December when the report comes out?

Mr. CRANE. It was—the NRC was pretty slow. It took several months. We haven't worked those issues out yet.

Mr. MICA. I have to study that some more.

Mr. Chairman, I have many additional questions, several pages, and I would ask unanimous consent or consent permission that they be submitted to these witnesses, and that they be allowed to respond, and it be made part of the record.

Mr. ZELIFF. Without objection, so ordered.

Mr. Clinger.

I guess I just have one or two here. And Dr. Rivolo, there is one thing that is bothering me, and it keeps nagging at me a little bit. Did I hear you say that you heard not a word of this is to get out?

Mr. RIVOLO. Yes, sir. Once the staff vehicle—right back to the Pentagon. That was my understanding, that until further notice, none of this was to get out, yes.

Mr. ZELIFF. That is not be suppressed or delayed or not be buried, just the word is——

Mr. RIVOLO. It was not a directive, but it was said, and, in fact, we canceled the briefing for the following day.

Mr. ZELIFF. I guess that my summation of this is that we are all here, and my friend Mr. Cummings on many occasions has talked about the drug situation in Baltimore. I represent New Hampshire. We have done Operation Street Sweeper in Manchester. It has very been effective. We are doing stuff in Nashua, in small towns. We have been with the Coast Guard in transit zone. We have been in source country programs.

We have worked very, very hard to put together the appropriate response to the administration's request. Admittedly, I think we did everything and more Barry McCaffrey, in terms of his office, not only the staffing of his office, but the appropriate resources that the administration feels they need.

Certainly in terms of cooperation, I think that we have been there and done it, and my concern is I have three grandchildren that I'm worried about. All of us have our kids that we are worried about, and this is an epidemic. Drug use all ages, all drugs are out of control, and particularly the most recent data that we had a hearing on last week where teenage drug use is out of control.

And I think that the only problem that I have with—or the major problem that I have with this thing is this information was given to us in a timely manner. If we could have effected some possible changes in the 1996 report, we could have effected changes in the 1997 appropriations, and when kids are dying on the streets, we don't have a year to waste. So I think the responsibility somewhere along the line has to be shared by all of us, all of us that allows that to happen, you all for allowing that to happen.

We have had a good discussion here for 2 hours. Hopefully we will hear some more with additional panels. I think it is an absolute tragedy to allow another year to go by. If, in fact, your data is good, hard research, and it is the right data, and it survives the daylight of being the right data, then we should have had that information. We shouldn't be messing around waiting for six more revisions so this gets the right words. I think everybody said look beyond the minor changes or whatever kind of changes you have been making in all of these drafts; the substance of the report still stands, and you are proud of it. Am I right in that, Dr. Crane? Am I right?

Mr. CRANE. Yes, sir.

Mr. ZELIFF. It is unfortunate we don't have that data as an oversight subcommittee here, as we who are committed to the drug czar's office and the President, to give them the resources they need to fight the war on drugs. It is an issue that affects all Americans. It is the most important serious issue that we face in this country today. And you combine drugs and crime together, I don't know of anything more important that we need to fight. We need all the information we can get to so we make the right decisions.

So on behalf of all of us—and I don't think there is anybody here that is not part of this—and those of us that couldn't be here today, we thank you for being here, and we may have not used the right words somehow, but I think the consensus here is that we need the information in that report as soon as we can get it. We need to be able to evaluate it, and if it is correct, we need to make the appropriate changes in our strategy.

Thank you all very much for being here. We will take a 5-minute recess while we await General McCaffrey and the next panel.

[Brief recess.]

Mr. ZELIFF. At this point I would like to welcome national drug czar, Gen. Barry McCaffrey.

General, we thank you for being here today.

General MCCAFFREY. Good to be here today.

Mr. ZELIFF. If you would please raise your right hand.

[Witness sworn.]

Mr. ZELIFF. Please be seated if you would.

I know you have had a chance to be watching some of this testimony, but if you would give us the condensed version of your opening statement, we would appreciate that, and obviously the balance of your statement will be included in the record.

STATEMENT OF GEN. BARRY McCAFFREY, DIRECTOR, OFFICE OF NATIONAL DRUG CONTROL POLICY

General McCAFFREY. Mr. Chairman, I thank you for the opportunity to come down here and discuss interdiction in general and also respond to your concerns about the IDA study in question.

With your permission, I will submit for the record my prepared comments, which include, I might add, all the briefing charts that are over here. I say that because I think this is the best synopsis not only of the IDA study, but also where we think Admiral Kramek and I and the rest of the interagency working group, where we are on the whole notion of interdiction.

Mr. ZELIFF. Without objection so ordered.

General McCAFFREY. If I may also begin by thanking the bipartisan leadership of both the Senate and the House for what we believe to be the final action on the drug budgets. Now, we have looked at the results, we think we have got not only what we asked for, but more, and I think it will take us a couple of weeks to sort it out. But if I may praise your leadership and others, Denny Hastert, and Rob Portman, Steny Hoyer, and Mr. Rangel and the many others in the House, and I call Senator Lott and Senator Daschle and thank them for their support. I think you have given us the tools to do our job, and indeed the 1996 budget which restored full funding to the Office of National Drug Control Policy did us a great service. We will put together the people, the men and women we need to manage this absolutely essential responsibility.

Now let me—if I may, I am going to go very briefly and just touch upon some elements of the argument that I would like you to consider. First of all, what we have done in the 1997 budget, and what I have done since I was sworn in on March 1, is to draft and support the national drug strategy. I had to ask the President and put it in front of the American people in Miami several months ago as a product—it got in late. By law it was supposed to be in on February 1. The Senate was pretty gracious about giving me a little latitude to work it over.

That is the National Drug Strategy, and I underscore it because I came from 2 years running the interdiction process of the United States in Southern Command. I have worked this issue since day one of this administration, and indeed in my last responsibility as a J–5 of the joint staff, worked it during President Bush's last year from the Pentagon, and when we wrote that drug strategy, we said fundamentally there can be no magic solution. There is no silver bullet, although there is absolutely one first priority, and that is to motivate America's youth to reject illegal drugs and substance abuse.

However, as you look at that strategy, you note that goals four and five fundamentally relate to what we are talking about today. It says we must—we owe the American people a defense of our air, land and sea borders, and that defense is not just the Customs Service, INS, Coast Guard, but an extended defense for it all the way into Burma and south into the cocaine-producing countries.

Then goal No. 5, and it was written very deliberately this way, we need to break foreign and domestic sources of drugs. In the end game, the ultimate victory would be that there were no illegal drugs available, and we would have operated against demand to reduce it.

I tell you this because I want you to understand at the outset that I am fundamentally in agreement with your own concerns expressed publicly and really the logic behind the IDA paper that says interdiction is an essential aspect of reducing drug abuse in America. I couldn't agree more, and that is why the next graph hopefully will be—I am going to skip by this and the next one. Just be aware the charts are available if you want to direct questions to Admiral Kramek or I. These are the transit zones for counterdrug forces and the source zone counterforces.

I have spent the last 3 years of my life working on this problem. I understand the interdiction and source country challenges. I have listened to the people in the region. I have made the rounds of every command and control facility from all the agencies here in the United States. I got the picture. It needs to be improved, but you ought to understand as you look at that that those are real work by thousands of men and women, by 3,000 flights a year out of the military, the CIA, Customs, Coast Guard, and others; that this is a tremendous effort involving National Guard airmen who are on the ground in Peru, Ecuador, Colombia, and almost in Venezuela; that it is a real effort, and we are very proud of it. It involves Joint Interagency Task Force South in Panama, which works for the Joint Interagency Task Force in Key West, FL, commanded by a Coast Guard standard, and we are doing pretty good.

Next graph: This is a tough one, but let me make sure you have got the note of what I am saying. I don't know what the truth is on the last 5 years of politics, but I do know the truth on the raw numbers on the drug budget, and that is the truth right there. That is what President Bush and Clinton turned in over those years. The requested budget and the enacted budget, I will tell you what comes out to me without question. Congress cut President Bush's drug budget and then Clinton's budget until this year, and each year the President, whoever it was, then requested in the following year the same level of funding to which had been cut.

So both the executive branch and the Congress wound down the combined funding to support interdiction and source country. You have to turn that around.

Mr. ZELIFF. General, let me ask you a question. Could you have one of your staffers just draw in roughly where—the funding that we just gave you? Where would that be in that chart?

General MCCAFFREY. Well, unfortunately, I don't have it on there, but what you are going to see is, you did exactly what I asked you to do and more. You have turned it around in this year's budget.

Mr. ZELIFF. Let's see if just to get—we just want to get a feeling for where that would be.

General MCCAFFREY. You funded us, I think, 15 points; 3–5, I think is what you are going to find you did.

Mr. ZELIFF. Which is in excess of the request.

General MCCAFFREY. Absolutely.

Mr. ZELIFF. So it comes up where Mr. Mica is, for example, who is drawing $200 million in addition to the request?

General MCCAFFREY. That's it. You can't——

Mr. ZELIFF. So we are heading in the right direction.

And for the record, I guess, if you would, Mr. Mica, if you would—he is the greatest staffer in the world here. Just draw for us—let's take 1992 for those that may not be able to see the chart.

General MCCAFFREY. If you would allow me, I would much rather have Mr. Kinney do the drawing in. And I say that for a couple of good reasons.

Mr. ZELIFF. Mr. Mica is very pleased.

General MCCAFFREY. Mr. Mica didn't do very well in the third grade on crayoning. I think he has got it too high.

But let me just say up front that this in the 1998 budget that I am now writing will be our opportunity to demonstrate our commitment to interdiction. So I thank you for it.

Mr. ZELIFF. I would just like to make one point, because funding is key here. If you could just show us 1992, with the marker, and 1993 and 1994 and 1995, 1996 and 1997, and let the record show that this administration and other administrations, that the funding comes from Congress, and Congress funded, I believe, when we took over control, we gave full support of President Clinton's drug war.

General MCCAFFREY. You actually cut him by 1 percent each year. It doesn't show up. It's too bad I didn't do that in a better way to demonstrate. You actually cut him 1 percent each year. But you are correct, your funding support for the administration's request, the last 2 years, have been good.

Mr. ZELIFF. I just wanted to make that as part of the record.

General MCCAFFREY. That's good. That's a good point.

Take that one down, if you will. Let me run through this, because I think they want to get to questions.

This chart here, like many data in the interdiction world, can be interpreted a bunch of ways, some of them harmful. You are looking at the worldwide production of cocaine. Some of these numbers are soft, but I think they are good enough for us to discuss the issue.

What you see here is that essentially somewhere between 800 and 1,000 tons is the production capacity of HEL annually, and then out of that, the good guys of the world, whether it is Peruvian cops, Bolivian UMOBAR, Colombians, or Detroit policemen, take some of it. We get, sort of, a third of the cocaine every year.

The U.S. authorities, whether it starts with the Coast Guard or back into the police forces of America, get another 100 tons plus. It goes up; it goes down. This year, it's up dramatically. We are doing pretty good in the first quarter of this year.

Now, here is how I would not interpret that chart: I would not interpret this to mean that, regardless of how much money you gave us on interdiction and source country, it didn't matter; it didn't make a difference. It seems to me there are a bunch of other factors that you ought to ask me about that affect our ability to get Peru, Bolivia, Colombia, Mexico, Burma, Afghanistan, to affect the drug supply and drug smuggling.

What I would also tell you is that that is hundreds of metric tons of cocaine. I put in my testimony, 450 metric tons in the last 4 years. It's 1,400 metric tons in the last 7 or 8 years that didn't end up in our schools and in our communities.

I think we are going to be careful in our language. Listening to the earlier testimony, I applaud U.S. law enforcement not only for breaking gangs, for breaking infrastructure, but also for taking kilograms of cocaine and heroin away from criminals. I think they ought to keep at it. When they do it, they reduce the potential addiction among young people in America.

Now, the next one—the three of them I didn't show, if I may just direct your attention, Mr. Chairman, and your colleagues' and those in the audience, because I passed these out, here are three pages of the great review of the IDA draft study. I am not going to put them up on briefing charts. You have them available. You are welcome to look at them and make of it what you would.

I would also hold up, just so you are aware I know about it, here is the document that I got in May. I actually didn't read it on that day. I read it about 2 weeks ago. And it is a draft document, unclassified, very complex work, by three brilliant men from a famous analytical institution in America, a nonprofit that comes out, calls the shots as best they can.

Now, my guess is—and what happened that day, essentially, I had Admiral Kramek, a close friend who I have worked with for years, came in with one of his officers and with—I think I had some of my people there; at a minimum, one. We get briefed on several issues. One of them was me briefing them on Mexico.

We talked about the interdiction conference. We talked about—Bob Kramek was about to start a big operation off Puerto Rico, Virgin Islands, he wanted to educate me on. Then finally, he and Captain Boyer briefed me in some detail about the IDA study. It was my view then that this was a loser of a proposition.

I said, along with Mr. Hastert, I taught economics for 3 years and I have an advantage over the analysts because I know I don't understand economics. I would like to have this study sent out to experts to see why what they are saying makes no sense to me as the soldier responsible for the interdiction campaign. Essentially they are telling me that, if you pour more resources into interdiction, that you will get this mathematical relationship reducing drug use.

What I was prepared to assert, and still do, is that if we had smart operations down there that followed the drug criminals to riverine coastal delivery, because every time you do something smart, they react, that it could be a valuable adjunct to our national drug policy. I say, get it out, send it out for study, and let's see how it stands up.

Neither—in my judgment, none of us intended to repress or delay or whatever, and, indeed, we went on, as you remember, to turn in a major request for additional funds, a $250 million supplemental, which included a lot of interdiction money. It also included a 43-percent increase in the 1997 budget for source-country programs. It included a 25-percent increase in funding for the southwest border, and it included a 9.3-percent increase in overall interdiction money.

So it was hardly the case that I saw a study whose magnificent logic so overwhelmed me that I persisted in not supporting interdiction. I am a prime advocate of that as one contribution to this drug strategy.

So the bottom line is, I think we have been unfair to IDA and to these three analysts by dragging them out in public on what should be a scientific debate over the validity of their work.

Now, I feel the same way about the RAND study. When it came out a year ago, it produced tremendous exchanges. It did influence thinking, and I am sure the IDA study will do the same thing, and we welcome it when they finally have it done.

On that note, Mr. Chairman, I am glad to be here and look forward to responding to your questions.

[The prepared statement of General McCaffrey follows:]

Barry R. McCaffrey
Director
Office of National Drug Control Policy
Executive Office of the President

Committee on Government Reform and Oversight
Subcommittee on National Security, International Affairs, and Criminal Justice
U.S. House of Representatives

October 1, 1996

I want to thank the Subcommittee for the opportunity to testify today about the role of interdiction in the *National Drug Control Strategy*. Interdiction is a key part of our strategy. We welcome the opportunity to highlight the important role interdiction plays in a balanced approach to reduce drug use and its consequences in America.

Interdiction: an integral part of the drug control strategy

It is important to note at the outset that interdiction is an important component of our integrated, systems approach to drug control, as set forth in the *1996 National Drug Control Strategy*. Interdiction is a vital complement to a balanced strategy that seeks to: motivate our youth to reject illegal drugs and substance abuse; to increase the safety of America's citizens by substantially reducing drug-related crime and violence; and to reduce the health, welfare, and crime costs resulting from illegal drugs. The *1996 Strategy* has five goals, two of which focus on interdiction.

GOAL 4: ***Shield America's air, land, and sea frontiers from the drug threat.***

Objective 1: Identify and implement options, including science and technology options, to improve the effectiveness of law enforcement to stop the flow of drugs into the United States, especially along the Southwest Border.

Objective 2: Lead efforts to develop stronger bilateral and multilateral intelligence sharing to thwart the use of international commercial air, maritime, and land cargo shipments for smuggling.

Objective 3: Conduct flexible interdiction in the transit zone to ensure effective use of maritime and aerial interdiction capabilities.

GOAL 5: ***Break foreign and domestic drug sources of supply.***

Objective 1: Destroy major trafficking organizations by arresting, convicting, and incarcerating their leaders and top associates, and seizing their drugs and assets.

Objective 2: Reduce the foreign availability of drugs through eradication and other programs that reduce drug crop cultivation and through enforcement efforts to attack chemical, money laundering and transportation networks that support trafficking organizations.

Objective 3: Reduce all domestic drug production and availability and continue to target for investigation and prosecution those who illegally divert pharmaceuticals and listed chemicals.

Objective 4: Increase the political will of countries to cooperate with the United States on drug control efforts through aggressive diplomacy, certification and carefully targeted foreign assistance.

Objective 5: Strengthen host nation institutions so that they can conduct more effective drug control efforts on their own and withstand the threat that narcotics trafficking poses to sovereignty, democracy and free-market economies. In the source countries, aggressively support the full range of host nation interdiction efforts by providing training and operational support.

Objective 6: Make greater use of multilateral organizations to share the burdens and costs of international narcotics control to complement the efforts of the United States and to institute programs where the United States has limited or no access.

Interdiction: A priority in principle and practice

The Administration requested $15.1 billion to implement the *1996 Strategy* in FY97, $1.4 billion of which will go towards interdiction efforts. Combined with what we spend on source nation support, the amount we spend on preventing illegal drugs reaching our country is $1.8 billion. This is considerably more than the amount spent in the peak "cocaine epidemic" years of 1982-86, when we estimated the nation had 5.7 million cocaine users; today that number is approximately 1.5 million. The percentage of the total drug control budget spent on interdiction has remained steady since 1995, while the percentage spent on demand reduction has actually declined. There is no question that interdiction is an important component of the strategy. Our challenge is to get the most out of these dollars.

Presidential review of cocaine interdiction efforts

After he took office in 1993, the President directed a review of our international drug control efforts in the Western Hemisphere. The result of that seven-month review, completed in November 1993, is referred to as the "source nation" strategy. It is a three-pronged effort to: (1) create and strengthen host nation institutions to give them the wherewithal to fight narco-traffickers with their own forces and resources; (2) target the leadership of the powerful drug cartels; and (3) implement a gradual shift of emphasis in interdiction from the transit zone to the source nations in the Andean Region. This was the right policy decision at the time and it remains an effective strategy today.

Source Country Efforts

Prior to assuming my position at ONDCP, I was the joint military commander responsible for and the principal architect of the Andean Ridge strategy. We devised interagency operations to implement the drug interdiction strategy. *Green Clover* was a superbly executed military operation which focused on disrupting the Peru/Colombia air bridge. Subsequently, *Operation Laser Strike* expanded the focus to include operations aimed at disrupting the riverine and coastal criminal drug smuggling. These operations achieved enormous tactical successes because of the professionalism and courage of the U.S. military elements which deployed to support allied police and military forces. The cooperative efforts of the U.S. country teams, the DEA, the U.S. Customs Service, the CIA, and our magnificent U.S. Coast Guard were fundamental to these gains. Perhaps the most important outcome was the team work and confidence we engendered with our hemispheric partners.

Despite interdiction funding below that requested, we have, over the past years, begun to see the initial signs of success with our source nation strategy. That source country strategy, of course, cannot be fully effective without the cooperation and commitment of host nations. In Peru we have seen a full-scale commitment to interdiction which resulted in the destruction of over 20 narco-trafficking aircraft in the past two years, many with intelligence or tracking assistance from the U. S. military forces coordinated by JIATF-South at Howard Air Force Base in Panama.

In Colombia, the Colombian Air Force has forced down and/or destroyed on the ground approximately 25 trafficker aircraft. Colombian law enforcement agencies have also seized almost sixty suspected narco-trafficking aircraft. The Colombian Police and Armed Forces have been superb partners in the past year despite enormous casualties and sacrifice.

Throughout the region, in the past year we have greatly increased our support to host nation interdiction efforts. On any particular day there are about 20 U.S. Coast Guard, Customs, and DOD aircraft involved in source country counterdrug operations. Approximately 300 additional military personnel are deployed in South America supporting *Operation Laser Strike*. These military personnel operate Ground Based Radar sites in remote Andean locations, fly detection and monitoring aircraft, and provide operational and intelligence support to our allies participating in this regional operation. Our AWACS, P3B's, SIGINT (Signals Intelligence), PHOTINT (Photographic Intelligence), and FLIR (Forward Looking Infrared Radar) aircraft all operate in complete prior coordination with regional governments and military authorities.

The results of this multinational, cooperative effort have yielded stunning tactical results. The so-called "air bridge" between Peru and Colombia saw a greater than 50 percent temporary reduction of flights as aircraft were intercepted and, in some cases, shot down. The cost of shipment increased fivefold as pilots demanded more money as their personal risk increased dramatically. Movement was reduced so drastically that there was a glut of coca base on the market and the price of the product being shipped fell by 50 percent overall and by as much as 80 percent in some areas.

Our challenges now are to: further restrict the movement of illegal drugs by air between Bolivia, Peru, and Colombia; block drug traffickers from developing alternate ground, river, and maritime routes; and to assist our South American partners in building the air and military capabilities necessary to defend their sovereign air, land, and sea space from incursion by international criminal drug organizations.

Conducting smarter interdiction operations in the transit zone.

In the transit zone, we continue to operate against well-funded, well-equipped, and increasingly sophisticated adversaries. Over the years we have maintained a robust capability in the transit zone through the cooperative efforts of the U.S. Armed Forces, the Coast Guard, Customs, the CIA, DEA, and allied nations. We orchestrate operations that are based on "cued" intelligence. We develop collaborative intelligence on drug smuggling activities which alerts us to probable drug movements and enables us to target specific ships, aircraft, and containers. Our tactical successes are forcing this criminal empire to move smaller shipments with greater cunning by new patterns.

Drug traffickers have shifted routes and become more sophisticated.

Seventy percent of the cocaine entering the United States comes across the Southwest Border; DEA estimates that the remainder comes through the Caribbean. Following our brilliant air and sea interdiction successes in the 1980s in the western Caribbean, criminal traffickers changed their modes of operations. They used to be able to fly twin-engine civil aviation aircraft from Colombia to small islands in the Bahamas and then air drop drugs into either Florida or our coastal waters for subsequent pick-up by fast boats. Their success was predicated on the "big sky" or "big ocean" theory and on our inadequate detection and monitoring capabilities. In response to this challenge, we developed extensive detection and monitoring capabilities to sort legitimate air and maritime traffic from illicit drug traffic. As our interdiction organizations and strategies became more effective, drug traffickers changed their routes and modes of transportation in response. The contributions of the ROTHR (Relocatable Over the Horizon Radars) elements in Texas and Virginia have been vital, as have been the U.S. Air Force Ground Based Radars in Colombia, Ecuador, and Peru. We need an additional ROTHR unit in Puerto Rico to complete the long range net. In addition, we rely heavily on the success of the CBRN (Caribbean Basin Radar Network).

We have, as a result of the combined efforts of the Armed Forces, Coast Guard, Customs, DEA, and cooperating governments in Central American and the Caribbean, mostly sealed the western Caribbean approach to drug aircraft and now face a new and perhaps even more complex problem. Cocaine traffickers are challenging our interdiction agencies by approaching the United States indirectly through the eastern Caribbean, and then into Puerto Rico, the Virgin Islands, the Mexico land route, and the eastern Pacific, or by hiding their drugs in commercial sea cargo shipments.

Puerto Rico is a natural point of entry because of its central location amidst major lines of communication in the Caribbean and the absence of customs inspections of what is, for all practical purposes, domestic cargo traffic between the island and the continental United States (CONUS). As a result of this increased drug trafficking activity, approximately seven tons of cocaine are smuggled each month into Puerto Rico, 80 percent of it destined for CONUS. Colombian drug traffickers find willing accomplices in the 200,000-300,000 illegal Dominican aliens residing in Puerto Rico. These traffickers charge only 20 percent of the cocaine they smuggle in payment, compared to the 50 percent often demanded by Mexican traffickers.

The consequences of this drug trafficking have been devastating to Puerto Rico. Cocaine sold in Puerto Rico is cheaper than anywhere else in the United States. Violent gangs control almost 1,000 drug distribution points throughout the island and victimize more than 300 public housing areas. The mean age of gang members is 14-17 years. Puerto Rico has a higher per capita murder rate than any other state or territory in the United States, and money laundering is big business there. Officially declared transactions by Dominican couriers in Puerto Rico in 1993 totaled $1.2 billion – 17 percent of the Dominican GNP.

To meet this challenge in the eastern Caribbean, the Customs Service recently began Operation Gateway, an interagency operation which features expanded maritime and air enforcement, heightened cargo examinations, and more frequent small vessel searches. The program is designed to close the U.S. back door to illicit drug smuggling. We also continue to conduct superb multinational counterdrug operations in the eastern Caribbean through agencies such as the Coast Guard and JIATF-East.

ONDCP recently established the Puerto Rico/U.S. Virgin Islands High Intensity Drug Trafficking Area (HIDTA) to confront the threat posed by international drug trafficking. The HIDTA program has formed 10 task forces and a supporting intelligence coordination center. The effort involves 26 agencies and over 600 Federal, State and local personnel who work to combat drug trafficking and related crimes (e.g. money laundering). The goal is to significantly disrupt drug trafficking and transshipment.

Although this HIDTA effort has only been in operation for eight months, several initial successes indicate that this interdiction effort will make a measurable impact on drug trafficking in the region. During FY96, this HIDTA reported that HIDTA participants arrested 417 individuals, confiscated 14,500 kg of cocaine, 11 kg of heroin, and 13,598 lb of marijuana, and seized $8 million in assets and currency. The leadership of Governor Rosselló and his senior prosecutors, law enforcement officials, and the National Guard have been instrumental to our growing successes. We have much more to do and will need more resources in coming years.

Southwest Border

Along the critical Southwest Border, we have beefed up our presence to confront the growing challenge of increased overland shipment. We have hardened physical barriers, such as with Operation Gatekeeper in San Diego. We are adding over 1500 personnel in the Border Patrol, Customs, DEA, FBI and the Department of Justice. We will continue to bolster our joint interdiction efforts along the Southwest Border. We will continue to work with Mexico to return the rule of law to our common border. To that end, we would hope to see the Border Patrol double by the year 2000.

The U.S. Armed Forces provides enormous support to this effort. More than 3,500 National Guard personnel are committed on a given day. Last year more than 10,000 active duty military personnel also joined in this interagency effort.

Our interdiction efforts are paying off

I would like to briefly review some of the results of our interdiction efforts.

- **Drug cartel leaders have been effectively targeted.**
  In the past year, the top seven leaders of the Cali cartel have been arrested in Colombia. Six remain incarcerated; one was killed by Colombian police resisting arrest after he escaped from prison. Jose Castrillon Henao, a major Panamanian cocaine trafficker, was arrested this summer and awaits trial in Panama. These arrests were the result of exhaustive, cooperative investigations conducted by multiple U.S. and Colombian agencies. Drug trafficking organizations are feeling the effects of the loss of this leadership. These successes also underscore that our international counterdrug programs represent an across-the-spectrum attack on drug trafficking operations. We are not only going after the leadership of these organizations, but we are hitting them where it hurts -- attacking their profits. We are going after narco-kingpins in the source countries, in the transit zone, and here at home.

- **International drug trafficking organizations are being broken up in the U.S.**
  A recent successful multi-agency case that was headed by the DEA and the FBI along with the Criminal Division of the Justice Department, and included 52 state and local police departments and other Federal agencies. This Southwest Border Initiative called Operation Zorro II, clearly illustrated the direct relationship of the international drug cartels in our violent domestic crime problem. In the Los Angeles High Intensity Drug

Trafficking Area, the Southern California Drug Task Force and 36 police departments synchronized their efforts as a team of task forces to focus on this complex operation centered in their area. In May of this year, the eight month investigation culminated in 156 arrests, the seizure of almost 56,000 kilograms of cocaine, and over $17 million.

- **U.S.-backed Colombian interdiction and eradication efforts are succeeding.** In Colombia this summer, in conjunction with *Operation Laser Strike*, the Colombian Army and National Police began aggressive operations in the coca and opium growing and production regions aimed at reducing cultivation, processing, and the introduction of precursor chemicals to the areas. Initial Colombian reports indicated over 150 cocaine labs destroyed and the almost total temporary disruption of the supply of precursor chemicals to the region. Press reports also indicated the exodus of many out of work cocaine laborers from cocaine producing regions and other signs of significant disruptions in the cocaine economy. The most significant indication that the cocaine industry in Colombia has been hurt is the large scale protests of cocaine workers. In some areas, as many as 20,000 protestors have been reported in the streets. Unfortunately, these efforts have also generated violent responses from narco-guerrillas. In the past month, rebels from the Revolutionary Armed Forces of Colombia (FARC) have conducted sophisticated and deadly assaults on military bases, police units, and infrastructure in the Guaviare Province in response to the eradication campaign.

The Colombian Armed Forces and National Police have clearly demonstrated their commitment to protecting their nation and its democratic institutions from the corrupting influence of narco-traffickers. We have been consistently impressed by this commitment and by the honesty of the Colombian Armed Forces, the National Police, and its director, General Serrano. These organizations deserve our continued support.

IDA Draft Study

During the 19 September 1996 hearing before this Subcommittee on heroin, concerns were raised regarding a draft study conducted by the Institute for Defense Analysis (IDA) for the Department of Defense as part of its ongoing review of drug interdiction efforts. This draft study, "An Empirical Examination of Counterdrug Interdiction Program Effectiveness," is a work in progress to analyze the cost effectiveness of U.S. international interdiction efforts.

During a briefing for ONDCP staff on the draft study by the authors, serious concerns were raised regarding the methodology used. ONDCP expressed strong doubts and recommended that IDA involve an economist in the analytical process. In addition ONDCP widely distributed the draft document to major research institutions for their comments on how the analysis might be improved. This is the same open peer review process employed by most academic journals prior to publication. Upon receipt of the draft study in May, ONDCP sent the paper to noted researchers in the field for a peer review at John F. Kennedy School of Government, Harvard University/BOTECH; Carnegie-Mellon Institute, University of Pittsburgh; University of Maryland/Rand Corporation, and Evidence Based Research.

The peer reviewers individually reached the same conclusions that the draft study: (1) contains serious methodological flaws; (2) reflects a poor understanding and use of drug-related data; (3) demonstrates an inadequate review of the literature; and (4) ignores the impact of the increased sentences for drug-related crime, and other law enforcement measures reflected in the various omnibus Federal crime and drug legislation over the past decade. It is worth noting several comments in particular:

- *The principal conceptual problem of the study lies in the claim that the retail price of cocaine would, in the absence of effective interdiction programs, have fallen to $25 per pure gram. This ignores all the other factors, particularly other federal and state enforcement programs that influence the price of cocaine and leads to a dramatic overstatement of the cost-effectiveness of interdiction.* (University of Maryland)

- *...the study is flawed by a failure to interpret a number of data series correctly...The misinterpretation of the DAWN and DUF series leads to baffling analyses...* (University of Maryland)

- *The study shows strikingly little familiarity with the relevant analytic literature.* (University of Maryland)

- *If I had been asked to review the IDA study for a journal, my recommendation to the editor would have been somewhere between "Reject" and "Revise and resubmit with no promise of publication," but leaning toward a flat rejection.* (Harvard University)

- *Some of the number-crunching is interesting, but the conceptual flaws are too deep to be remedied in any straightforward way; they'd have to start from scratch and write a different paper. Moreover, the authors fail to display the familiarity with the background on drug-market economics that would be needed to get the study right.* (Harvard University)

- *It is clearly fundamentally flawed in its approach and conclusions and reads as if the authors were neither well versed in the drug policy literature nor in the standard social sciences, particularly economics.* (Carnegie-Mellon Institute)

It turns out that IDA conducted its own internal review of the draft study *after* receiving the peer reviews conducted for ONDCP. IDA concludes that:

- *Several analytical excursions need to be eliminated from the paper.*

- *Fix the price series. If the result are the same, claim the correlation, but be more modest about the causation and look for other supporting data. Eliminate all unnecessary analyses...*

- *This* [The impact of source-zone interdiction enforcement on supply] *seems highly plausible, but the authors offer no quantitative evidence of this assertion...*

- *Here* [Retail price increases] *the debate over the IDA analysis is confused by the introduction of unnecessary -- either overstated or just plain silly -- arguments.*

- *A clear failing of the IDA paper is the lack of a well-articulated model of the dynamics of the cocaine market, of how supply disruptions might work their way through this market, and of the goals of an anti-drug policy.*

IDA's internal review finds much of the peer review conducted for ONDCP to be right on point:

- *...the reviewers are quite correct in noting that the IDA analysis offers no evidence in support of the assertion that source-zone interdiction explains any of the difference between the project price floor ($25) and the observed price floor (slightly more than $50).*

And IDA's internal review finds that the draft study's authors lack an adequate economic analysis of the issue:

- *The first thing I learned in my first econometrics course is that* correlation does not imply causation.

- *...the IDA analysts show no apparent understanding of the distinction between movement* along *a demand curve and the movement* of *a demand curve. ...it is one of the first things taught in econometrics classes, and is thus the kind of rookie mistake that unnecessarily undermines the credibility of the rest of the analysis.*

Rather than having "suppressed" the IDA draft study ONDCP has shared the report widely to provide feedback on the draft, and to ensure that it was subjected to the kind of peer review necessary for an analysis to have credibility. IDA is a good analytical institution and the authors well intentioned. It is unfortunate that the frank scholarly discourse which is routinely generated during the preparation of a complex study such as this has been publicized before the researchers were able to take critical peer reviews into account to improve their work.

<u>We need your partnership and support</u>

- **Interdiction works.**
  Our comprehensive interdiction efforts are effective. Interdiction clearly works. It is an important element of a comprehensive balanced counterdrug strategy. In the past four years, U.S. agencies alone have seized 475 metric tons of cocaine. These seizures are expensive to the traffickers. Our successes hurt them. The sobering news is that only about a third of the cocaine in the pipe-line is seized by international law enforcement. This has been the consistent trend for the past several years. We also face other emerging challenges. According to Interpol, global production potential of heroin reached a record high last year of 450 metric tons; however, only 37 tons were seized worldwide in 1995. The U.S. demand for heroin is currently about 10 tons, approximately two percent of the global production potential.

- **Our strategy is sound.**
  It is critical to implement the *1996 National Drug Control Strategy* with its balanced approach to the supply and demand aspects of the problem. The FY97 counterdrug budget increases our interdiction resources by 7.3 percent, and increases our international programs by 25.4 percent. These increases provide for meaningful reinforcement of our agencies and bureaus serving on the Southwest Border and will strengthen our already effective efforts in South America and in the Caribbean.

- **We should be optimistic.**
  ONDCP is optimistic about our interdiction posture. The Federal effort is better organized. Federal, State and local enforcement cooperation has never been better. Our agents and officials have been learning by doing. As a nation, we are finally paying adequate attention to the problems created by the illegal drug trade along our Southwest Border. Our Allies, in particular Peru and Mexico, are clearly dedicated to protecting their people and democratic institutions from this terrible criminal threat.

- **We should also be realistic.**
  We should also be realistic about the magnitude of the challenge of shielding our air, land, and sea frontiers from the drug threat. Drug traffickers will probe any weakness along our 5,525 mile-long borders with Canada or our 1,933 mile-long border with Mexico. They will seek to introduce drugs over our 12,000 miles of coastline. They will consider using our 13,228 airports and hiding couriers among the more than 60 million air passengers that enter the U.S. each year. They will attempt to hide drugs in the more than 400 million tons of imports that enter the U.S. through our 50 busiest seaports each year -- the cocaine they traffic represents less than one millionth of that volume. They will also seek to use the nine million containers that enter the U.S. to hide their drugs.

Demand reduction as a partner of interdiction.

We cannot protect the American people by relying principally on interdiction to solve the drug problem. We must coordinate our demand reduction efforts with domestic law enforcement, international cooperation, and interdiction efforts. We must take the profit out of narcotics trafficking through asset forfeiture and attacks on money laundering. We must confront domestic and foreign corruption caused by drug money. We must reduce the cost of drug abuse to America. **This is why the first priority goal of the Drug Strategy will remain:** ***to motivate America's youth to reject illegal drugs and substance abuse.***

We have seen enormous success in persuading Americans to reject drugs. Overall drug abuse in America is down by 50 percent in the last 15 years. While the number of cocaine users in America has dropped by 75 percent, the amount of cocaine produced worldwide and entering America has remained relatively constant. Therefore we continue to see great tragedies of addicts using more cocaine with its terrible personal and social consequences. The good news is that there just isn't that large a market in the number of cocaine users anymore. The bad news is that a significant number of Americans remain chronically addicted to cocaine and heroin, and many are incarcerated for reasons related to drugs.

If we can motivate America's youth to reject cocaine and other drugs, our interdiction programs will be enhanced. Fewer drug smugglers will be willing to run the interdiction gauntlet for a reduced payoff. Every shipment we seize will hurt the smugglers that much more.

We Need Your Help

The *National Drug Control Strategy* is not a partisan plan. It needs your bipartisan support to enable the nation to sustain a concerted effort against illegal drugs and their consequences.

The Strategy relies on partnerships between the United States and our allies, among various Federal agencies, and between State and local agencies and the Federal government. For the *Strategy* to succeed, we must achieve a partnership among the Congress, the Executive Branch, and the American people. Together we can protect our children.

There are no quick fixes to this problem. ONDCP looks forward to working with Congress to develop comprehensive, long range plans to deal with drug abuse. We need to develop a five-year budget, and a ten-year strategy to both sustain and expand our successes. Most importantly, we need to work together.

It is an honor for me to continue to serve the United States national security interests as the Director of the Office of National Drug Control Policy. I have been wounded in combat three times serving America in three conflict situations. During my 36 years in uniform, I have not encountered a greater threat to the health of the American people than that posed by illegal drugs. I ask for your support and wisdom.

Office of National Drug Control Policy
FY 1997 National Drug Budget

Total Budget 9.3% Increase (largest in history)

Prevention/Education increases 11.3%
(40 million school children/97% school districts)

Treatment increases 8.6%
–Treats 1.1 million/3.6 million need
–$100 million proposed for Drug Courts
–Treatment for State/Federal prisoners

Law Enforcement increase 9.3%
–Expanded DEA/FBI targeting organizations
–2,000 more police under COPS
–2,420 more prison beds

Interdiction/SW Border increases 7.3%
–More than 1,500 staff for SWB
–25% increase Border Patrol

$15.1 Billion President's Request

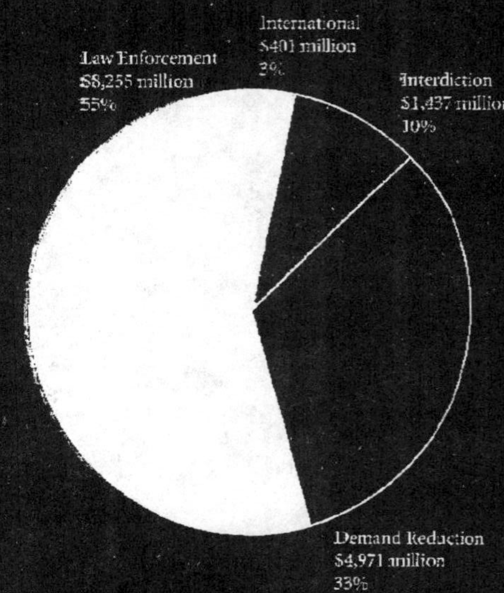

ONDCP
September 1996

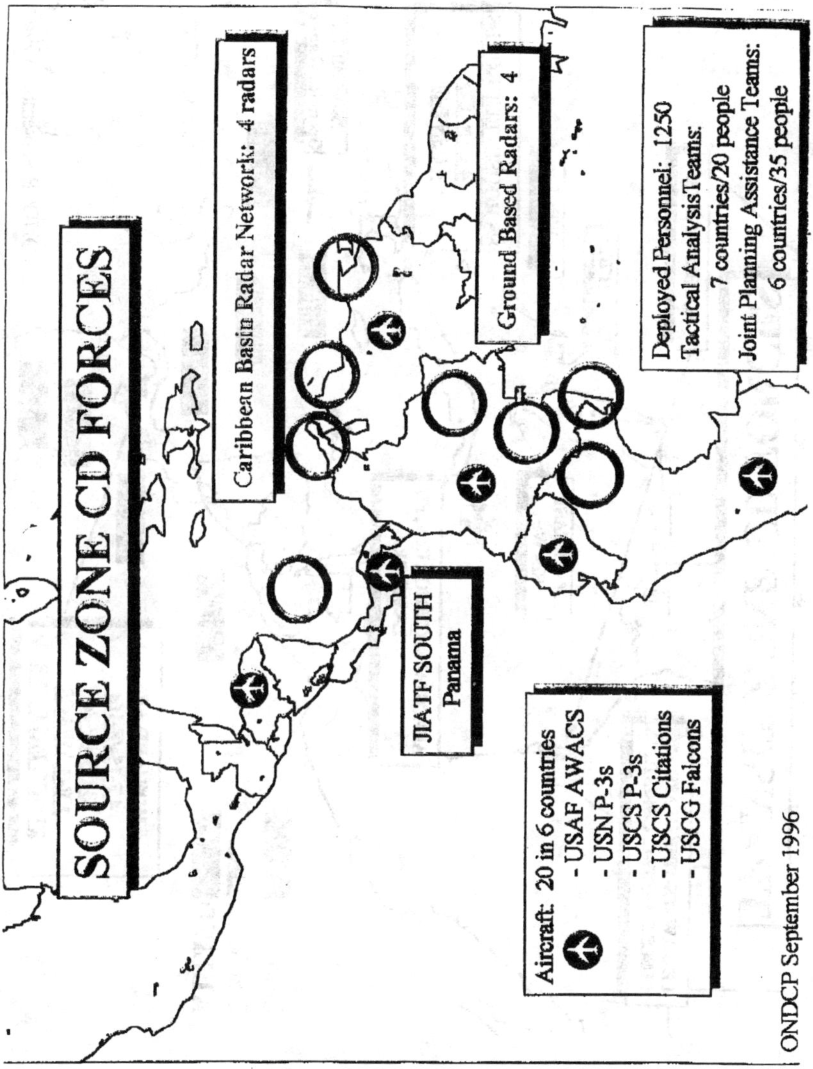
SOURCE ZONE CD FORCES
Caribbean Basin Radar Network: 4 radars
JIATF SOUTH
Panama
Ground Based Radars: 4
Aircraft: 20 in 6 countries
- USAF AWACS
- USN P-3s
- USCS P-3s
- USCS Citations
- USCG Falcons
Deployed Personnel: 1250
Tactical AnalysisTeams:
7 countries/20 people
Joint Planning Assistance Teams:
6 countries/35 people
ONDCP September 1996

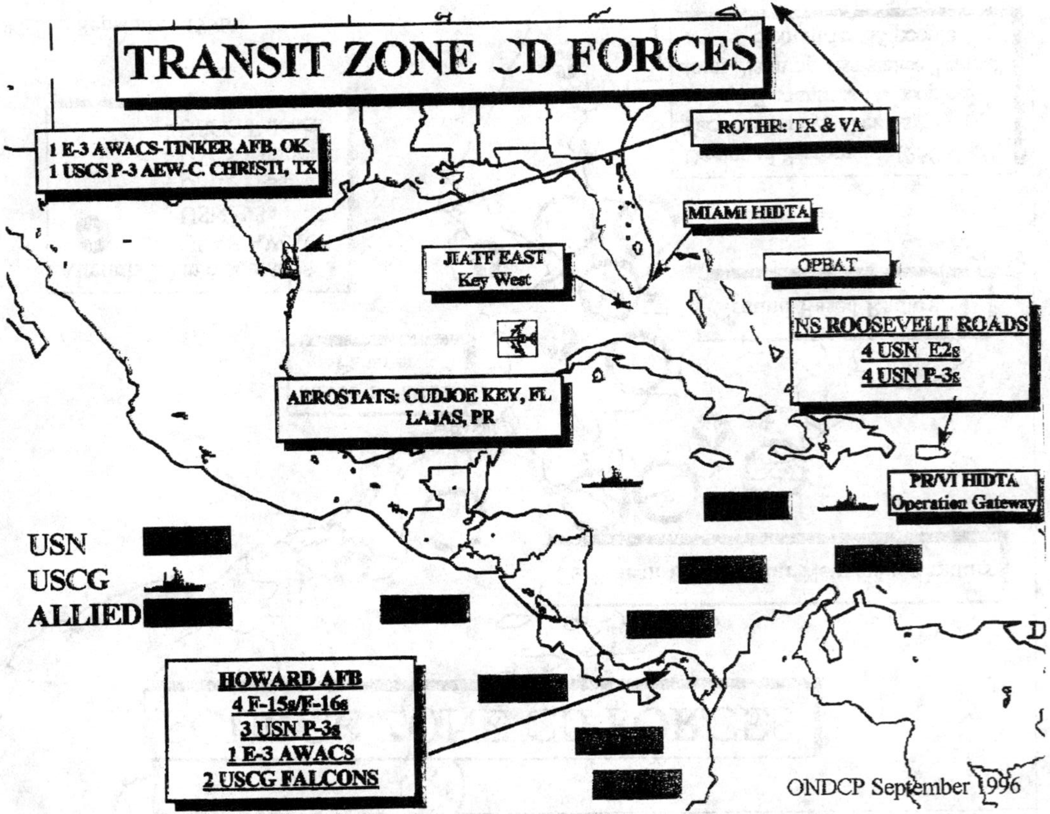
TRANSIT ZONE CD FORCES
1 E-3 AWACS-TINKER AFB, OK
1 USCS P-3 AEW-C. CHRISTI, TX
ROTHR: TX & VA
MIAMI HIDTA
JIATF EAST
Key West
OPBAT
NS ROOSEVELT ROADS
4 USN E2s
4 USN P-3s
AEROSTATS: CUDJOE KEY, FL
LAJAS, PR
PR/VI HIDTA
Operation Gateway
USN
USCG
ALLIED
HOWARD AFB
4 F-15s/F-16s
3 USN P-3s
1 E-3 AWACS
2 USCG FALCONS
ONDCP September 1996

International and Interdiction Resources: Request versus Enacted Budgets

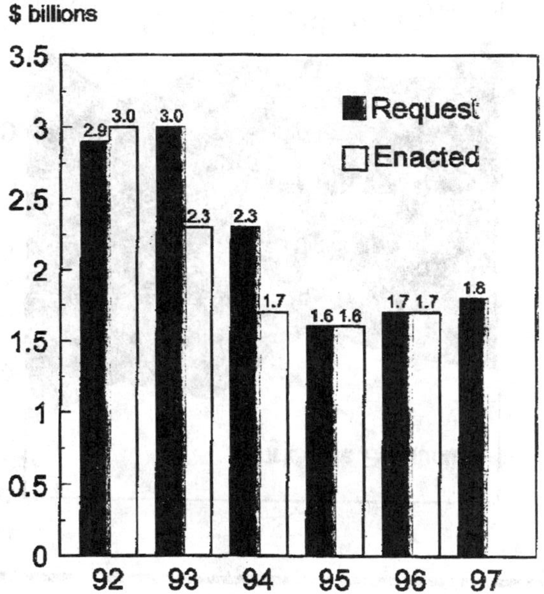

Over the 1992 - 1996 time period, Congressional cuts have totaled $1.3 billion, or 11 percent, less than Bush and Clinton Administration requests.

Congress cut Bush Administration FY 93 request by 24 percent.

Congress cut Clinton Administration FY 94 request 27 percent.

Congress cut Clinton Administration FY 95 request 2 percent.

Congress cut Clinton Administration FY 96 request 1 percent.

ONDCP

Cocaine Seizures versus Production

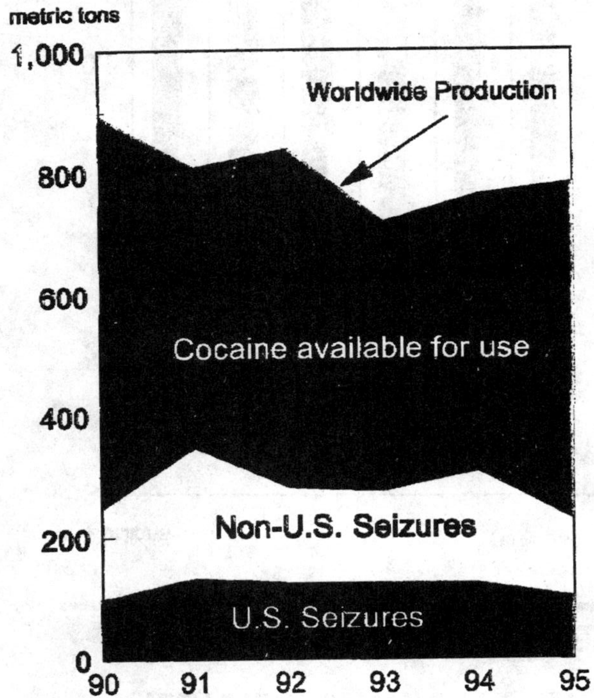

U.S. and foreign governments interdict about one-third of worldwide cocaine production:

Worldwide production has ranged generally between 800 to 900 metric tons since 1990.

U.S. cocaine seizures have averaged 113 metric tons per year over the 1990 to 1995 period.

Foreign government seizures have averaged 168 metric tons over the same period.

U.S. cocaine seizures are up in 1996 -- 26 metric tons of cocaine were seized in the first quarter of 1996, up 4 percent compared to the first quarter of 1995.

ONDCP

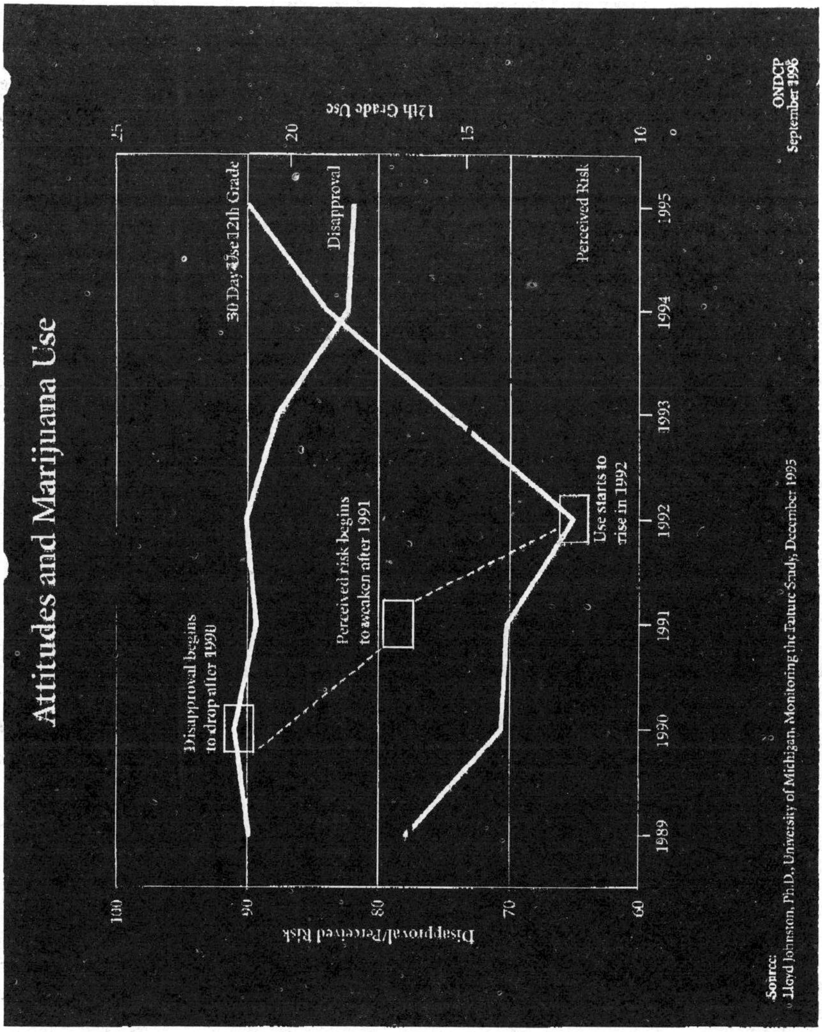
Attitudes and Marijuana Use
Disapproval/Perceived Risk
100
90
80
70
60
12th Grade Use
25
20
15
10
1989
1990
1991
1992
1993
1994
1995
Disapproval begins to drop after 1990
Perceived risk begins to weaken after 1991
Use starts to rise in 1992
30 Day Use 12th Grade
Disapproval
Perceived Risk
Source:
Lloyd Johnston, Ph.D., University of Michigan, Monitoring the Future Study, December 1995
ONDCP
September 1996

Mr. ZELIFF. Thank you, General McCaffrey.

Let me just start out on page 313 of your National Drug Control Strategy. I just refer you to the interdiction section, which I guess shows a high of $2 billion plus in 1991; $1.960 million in 1992; $1.511 million in 1993; $1.311 million in 1994; $1.280 million in 1995; $1.339 million in 1996. I guess my concern, as I did my wrap-up comments of the last panel, I am just worried that we may have lost a year here.

As we are questioning whether we are doing the right thing, are we doing the right mix? Are we putting the right resources in the right areas? Are we putting too much reliance on treatment of hard-core addicts and not enough on source-country programs?

If I take you down to the lower piece in the international, in 1991, it's $633 million; in 1992, $660 million; in 1993, $523 million; 1994, $329 million; 1995, $295 million. And so I guess my concern here, is that as we are in the process of putting the 1996 plan together and we are looking at the appropriations for 1997—I am just worried that someone in your position, and certainly in our position because we want the same information, we want to know, are we right about trying to push and beef up a little bit on interdiction?

Certainly our trip verified the fact that, with a little bit more, we could do so much more. And I think you agreed with that when we came back. So I just think it is valuable information that we have been denied if, in fact, we were denied it.

I would like to have the recorder, or reporter, play back one phrase or two from the previous panel and then have you respond to that, the part that not a word of this is to get out.

General MCCAFFREY. I would be glad to accept whatever your characterization was.

Mr. ZELIFF. I would like her to play it. Just let her play it back. It is the Clinger statement. I thought you had talked to her.

General MCCAFFREY. Mr. Chairman, I would be glad to accept whatever you tell me.

Mr. ZELIFF. What I would like to do—I guess you switched reporters in the meantime. So can you get that statement?

We will move on from that then, if you could pull that together.

I think what, general, was said, is that not a word of this is to get out. Apparently there was some rather heated discussion between you and Admiral Kramek relative to either whether you wanted to see the rest of this report or whether you did want to hear the report, whether you didn't want to hear the report.

Can you just bring us up to date as to how you remember that whole situation as it took place? And just help us a little bit. Guide us through the process.

General MCCAFFREY. Yes, sir, I would be glad to.

The—I don't believe there's any truth that any language was used: Not a word of this to get out. I think, indeed, it was supposed to get out to be widely reviewed by other scientific authorities.

I believe the report had been going on long before I got there. I believe the report first came up to ONDCP sometime in January. I don't know how I would characterize how it was received. I think it had been going on earlier in the preceding year.

Mr. ZELIFF. We were told, I guess, it was March.

General McCAFFREY. March of?

Mr. ZELIFF. This year.

General McCAFFREY. Well, now, the first time it came up to ONDCP was January, several months before I was sworn in. Then the first time I heard it was when Admiral Kramek and Boyer briefed me on it.

Mr. ZELIFF. Then did you hear the whole report?

General McCAFFREY. Well, the whole report—I got a briefing out of Boyer and Kramek.

Mr. ZELIFF. Did you get a briefing? OK.

General McCAFFREY. A pretty good briefing. They are smart guys. They know all about the business. They laid out the thinking.

I didn't like it. It seemed to me then and now that it was too much of a stretch to go from Laser Strike, which I was running, and Green Clover, to driving up prices of cocaine and demand down. So I said, that doesn't make any sense.

In addition, I was aware that there really hadn't been any change in price of cocaine in America. Use—price wasn't up; demand wasn't down. So I said, "You are giving us way too much credit."

What we can do in interdiction on the Air Bridge, and were doing quite successfully, is, we can make them react to us, go to a different form of smuggling, penetrate their systems with our intelligence while they do it, and drive up the tactical cost of delivery. That's what I thought we were doing.

Mr. ZELIFF. So you feel that that whole report was, to use the words that were given to you, utter nonsense, garbage, inappropriate?

General McCAFFREY. Well, I wish I had used more moderate language. I retract that. I think these are bright guys. It has value to hear other viewpoints. It certainly didn't ring too well with the scientific community when they saw it.

Mr. ZELIFF. Let me ask you this: Do you agree with the substance of the report?

General McCAFFREY. No, not at all.

Mr. ZELIFF. Nothing in the report at all?

General McCAFFREY. No, no. Wait. I think what I would agree with is that good interdiction pays off and that if you can get beyond Air Bridge operations, and Gen. Wes Clark now is moving into riverine coastal, and if we can get more effective support for Peruvian police and army, and if we can do alternative development better, then we will make a substantial contribution, and that will eventually affect drug use in America.

Mr. ZELIFF. Well, how would you describe the interdiction efforts that were taking place prior to 1993, up through 1992? Say, just for the 3 or 4 years, were they effective?

General McCAFFREY. Oh, yes. No, I think there was some brilliant work done by President Bush and the administration in responding to the initial threat, which was essentially drugs coming from Peru and Bolivia to Colombia and then directly into south Florida, Louisiana, and Texas. They got their act organized. They put a lot of machinery out in the Caribbean, and it worked.

Mr. ZELIFF. Did we learn anything from the fact when we stopped it and gutted that program—did we learn anything from the fact that it may have been premature?

General MCCAFFREY. Well, of course, we always do. But I guess what I tell you is, the threat changed. There was no drop in cocaine coming into America at all. It just moved through Mexico, and it kept coming, and purity and availability and price got worse, not better.

Now, having said that, I do not mean to imply it was useless. It wasn't useless. One thing it did was, it kept democratic governments in office in Latin America. Second, it stripped off hundreds of tons of cocaine. Third, there was a principle involved that we owe the American people a defense of our children.

So it was a brilliant effort. It caused them to respond, and now we have got to respond to their new patterns of smuggling and criminal behavior.

Mr. ZELIFF. Mr. Cummings.

Mr. CUMMINGS. Thank you very much, Mr. Chairman.

General McCaffrey, welcome.

I was just looking at some testimony that you gave back on September 19 during a hearing entitled, "Heroin, a Re-emerging Threat." Do you remember that before this committee? You may not remember.

General MCCAFFREY. Yes, heroin, yes.

Mr. CUMMINGS. Heroin, that's right.

General MCCAFFREY. Absolutely.

Mr. CUMMINGS. And during that, on page 87, lines 2009, you commented on this—all of what we are talking about today, this report, I think, as a response to one of Mr. Mica's questions. And you said, in part, "But the studies"—and I am quoting: "But the studies seem to imply that the interdiction campaign that I had run had achieved phenomenal successes in driving up the price of heroin and cocaine and reducing consumption. Personally, I found those conclusions utter nonsense, and so I asked them to be submitted in more of a scientific analytical process, which is what I think is happening now."

Is that—would that be accurate? Do you recall that?

General MCCAFFREY. Yes, I think that's a fair statement.

Mr. CUMMINGS. Is that the same thing you are saying today?

General MCCAFFREY. Yes, sir.

You know, Mr. Constantine, whose judgment I rely on a lot as a straight-talking cop, we didn't think the price of cocaine was going up in America because of our very successful interdiction operations. What we thought we were doing, we were killing criminals; we, the Peruvian Air Force, and the Colombians; we were doing great eradication work, and we were putting up a spirited defense which was causing them to change to a less effective smuggling system by river and by coastal freighter. And that's what they are trying to do right now.

Mr. CUMMINGS. You—in answering the chairman's questions a few minutes ago, you talked about this report, and I think you basically were saying that you felt like it was an honest effort.

I am going to quote again from that September 19 hearing transcript, and at page 87, lines—starting at line—I will start at line

2021. I just wonder if you recall this testimony back on September 19. Mr. Mica asked you a question.

This was critical of the first 2 years of the administration, and, in fact, did you try—you don't think you then tried to repress making that report public?

And this is your response at line 2027: "No, I don't think so. I think our attempt ought to be to apply cold, hard logic, and I interpreted that study to be honest as more—I interpreted that study to be an apology for increased machinery out in the Caribbean as opposed to confronting the drug issue."

Do you recall saying that?

General MCCAFFREY. Yes, I do. And let me put it in context. The last thing I want to do, as a fellow who believes in interdiction, is to go out in the street with a study that is immediately subject to attack as being a rented piece of paper that's supporting my position.

Now, I don't think that's what IDA was doing, but that was my concern, that I appear with a piece of paper that wouldn't withstand scrutiny, and that's the way I still feel about it.

Mr. CUMMINGS. General McCaffrey, there were some statements that have been from this bar—and I call it a bar; I guess it's just a table—about you. And I want to—since you didn't have a chance to defend yourself, I just want you to respond.

Once again, for the record, did you ever instruct Admiral Kramek or anyone to bury the draft interdiction report by the IDA?

General MCCAFFREY. No.

Mr. CUMMINGS. You never did?

General MCCAFFREY. No.

Mr. CUMMINGS. And you understand that you are sworn to tell the truth?

General MCCAFFREY. I certainly do.

Mr. CUMMINGS. Now, do you personally have any evidence that the price of cocaine on American streets is skyrocketing because of your efforts during your tenure——

General MCCAFFREY. No.

Mr. CUMMINGS [continuing]. To stop it?

General MCCAFFREY. No. Too bad. It hasn't. That does not imply that our efforts did not provide a tremendous boost to the counterdrug effort. It just didn't—what it did affect was the price of moving the drug. It killed some criminals and put a bunch of them in jail. It locked up most of the Cali Drug Cartel. It started a tremendous eradication program in Colombia, and it was a substantial contribution, at the risk of life, of a bunch of Air Force, Army, Navy, Coast Guard, agency, and other personnel. That's what we were doing.

Mr. CUMMINGS. Did you ever intimidate—to your knowledge, issue any kind of instructions that might be viewed as intimidation with regard to this report to anyone?

General MCCAFFREY. Admiral Kramek is pretty hard to intimidate. I don't think so.

Mr. CUMMINGS. As a matter of fact, back on September 19, you said that you had the utmost respect for Admiral Kramek, did you not?

General McCAFFREY. I think he is one of the finest people I have met in Government service and frequently the voice of reason in this whole process over the last 3 years that I have been working with him.

Mr. CUMMINGS. As a matter of fact, I direct your attention to our September 19, 1996, transcript from that September 19 hearing, and in response to one of Mr. Mica's questions, you, in commenting on Bob Kramek, you said: "Mr. Congressman, I don't—and I," at 2684, line 2684: "Mr. Congressman, I don't know. I believe Bob Kramek, who is probably one of the smartest, most able people in Washington, DC, I deal with, I believe he did, as the interdiction coordinator."

Do you still believe—I guess the part of that that I am most concerned about is the whole thing that you believe in his integrity and his brilliance. Is that right?

General McCAFFREY. Absolutely.

Mr. CUMMINGS. And you still hold that opinion?

General McCAFFREY. Yes; when we had—when we had the notion of an interdiction coordinator and a commandant of the Coast Guard was selected, there was a collective sigh of relief all over the system, because we trust the Coast Guard and we respected Admiral Kramek.

Mr. CUMMINGS. One last question, I think. General McCaffrey, can you please tell the subcommittee what the administration's position on interdiction is? Does not the administration believe that interdiction is an important component in stopping the use of illegal drugs in the United States?

General McCAFFREY. It is a vital component, and indeed it probably deserves even more resources in the years to come if we can intelligently apply them to the task and understand that these are tactical efforts that must be part of a coherent national strategy.

Mr. CUMMINGS. Thank you very much.

Mr. ZELIFF. Thank you, Mr. Cummings.

Mr. Clinger.

Mr. CLINGER. General McCaffrey, we had testimony earlier this morning that would appear to be in conflict with some of the statements that you have made here this afternoon. I just want to try and clarify those inconsistencies and, if there are, give you an opportunity at least to respond.

General McCAFFREY. Certainly.

Mr. CLINGER. We had an indication—you indicated that your briefing on this report was basically by Admiral Kramek, and I guess he was the one whom you discussed this with.

The question I have is: Did you, as has been indicated, refuse a briefing by the authors of the report after knowing of the conclusions of the study? In other words, you apparently had been briefed on the conclusions. The suggestion is that you were unwilling to meet with the people who actually wrote the report. In other words, you were getting a secondhand impression of the report. Did you refuse to meet with them?

General McCAFFREY. Yes, sir.

Well, let me just tell you that Captain Boyer talked through the briefing, using slides. Kramek and I had a discussion of it, and I think I used words to the effect that I didn't have time to wallow around in another hour of it; get it out for scientific review. I sort of think that's what I said.

Mr. CLINGER. Which implied, then, that you didn't have the time to really meet with the—or discuss the matter with the authors of the report?

General MCCAFFREY. That's correct.

Mr. CLINGER. Finally, I think this—you have been asked this a couple of ways, but the exact words, we understood, and I don't think you have been asked this, did you ever say to Admiral Kramek expressly, as others have testified, under oath this morning, that, quote, not a word of this study is to get out?

General MCCAFFREY. That would imply that I had never existed in Washington, DC, Mr. Clinger. I don't know of a report that doesn't get out.

Mr. CLINGER. That is true.

General MCCAFFREY. I sent the report out all over the country, to Harvard, Maryland, RAND Corp.

Mr. CLINGER. So you are saying, basically, no, you never said that? Is that right?

General MCCAFFREY. That's correct.

Mr. CLINGER. Now, obviously, my main interest in this is from the vantage point of the chairman of the full committee having to do with oversight of the Government as a whole. And would you agree that this report, and the form it was presented, would have been appropriate for the Congress, this committee or the Congress, to have in making deliberations in terms of resource allocation on the war on drugs?

I mean, it presented a conflicting point of view to the report that was relied upon by the administration in making the request, as I understand it, for resources. But I think that—would you agree that we should have had access to a contrary suggestion that the resource allocation was skewed, that, in fact, the emphasis was being given to the wrong side of the equation?

General MCCAFFREY. Mr. Clinger, I would agree with one thing. There is nothing in ONDCP, now or in the future, to which I will not give Congress ready access. There is no information that you shouldn't have access to.

The real question——

Mr. CLINGER. But we can only get it if we know that it exists.

General MCCAFFREY. Well, the real question is, should I give you something, a work in progress, a draft report that I hear for 10 minutes and to which I do not agree? As one of the experts on interdiction, even though I support interdiction, should I have sent this over saying, I don't agree with this thing, it's out for scientific review, but I wanted you to get it right away?

I don't know. I will do whatever is in Congress' best interest. But the quick answer is, no. I don't agree with the report then. And when I finally get it, I will take it into account, and if I don't agree with it, you will get to express your views to me since you own the purse strings.

Mr. CLINGER. So your view, then, is, it could only be made available to us, even though it was going to come after the fact in terms of the use we might make of it, if it was in a final report and had been studied—again, it had been studied for a year and a half.

General McCAFFREY. Yes.

Mr. Clinger, I don't know that anybody would ever keep this from you anyway. It is an unclassified study, and, you know, I would—our doors are open to you and your committee, and your staffers could go look at anything we are doing, because I also learn a lot from dealing with you all.

So I don't—I don't have a bit of problem with you having access to any documents over here, but I don't agree with this one, yet.

Mr. CLINGER. You can understand there's a bit of skepticism on our part here, because when you came into the office, you indicated you were going to produce a new drug strategy within 6 months. This report was available to you shortly after you came in. It, in fact, does basically repudiate or at least seriously question the previous three drug strategies that have been pursued by this administration.

So you can understand our skepticism that perhaps the motivation for this was, in fact, to substantiate what was going on, and which you ultimately did, and was undercutting what the administration had been pursuing for the previous 3 years, which apparently it was a failed policy.

General McCAFFREY. Well, Mr. Clinger, this report, if I completely agreed with it, would have been a wonderful bouquet for me personally to add to that strategy. This does not refute the strategy; it supports it. I think it's a weak read, so I am a little careful about going out and waving that document and saying, for that reason, give me goal 4 and $5.

Mr. CLINGER. It does, however, take on head-on the RAND study. I mean, it really is very critical and very condemnatory, if you will, of the RAND study.

General McCAFFREY. Yes, sir.

Mr. CLINGER. You sort of reject—think the RAND study was accurate in all respects and this was not?

General McCAFFREY. Wait a minute. I haven't talked about the RAND study. I don't really, to be honest, think that's an enormous contribution to the policy process either. What I believe is that you must, as a first priority, have young Americans reject illegal drugs.

Second, you have got to go to the addicted population, 3.6 million of whom are in the criminal justice system, and provide effective treatment. And then, in addition, you have got to go out and defend America's air, land, and sea frontiers and work with our democratic allies.

So I am fully supportive of this balanced strategy. And the RAND study—and again, I say this as an undergraduate engineer, not physicist—didn't lend itself to that dialog either. It implied you could ignore interdiction and go work the treatment. I don't think that's sensible, either.

Mr. CLINGER. Let me just say, in conclusion, you have talked about cooperation, and I think there has been very good cooperation between your office and this subcommittee over the last 2 years, under Chairman Zeliff's leadership and so forth. My concern and my disappointment was that this appeared to me, at least, and I think to others, that there was an element of suppression here which would belie the stated goals of cooperation.

I think if we don't have access to all of the information that we need to make these kinds of judgments, then that is not cooperation. So to that extent, I would express my disappointment that that cooperation, in my view, broke down on this issue.

General MCCAFFREY. Well, I respect your viewpoint. I am sensitive to it, and I will try and work harder to maintain your confidence.

Mr. ZELIFF. Mr. Hastert.

Mr. HASTERT. Thank you, Mr. Chairman.

Let me just set the record straight, general. Your first meeting with me was, I think, in March or late February of last year. Really, it was an inspiration for me to get involved in this whole drug interdiction process. And I have had a lot of hats in this Congress as chief deputy whip and lining up votes and doing health care, and sometimes I didn't need an extra job, but I took that on because I thought you were very sincere in our discussion. It was at a breakfast that Mr. Zeliff hosted, if I remember right.

Now, one of the things that, after our discussion and after a subsequent trip—I guess I would be what Mr. Mica might call a Johnny-come-lately to this issue, but I did get involved, at the Speaker's request, because we wanted to do the right thing. A lot of the trends that we were talking about were certainly trends that were set long before you became the drug czar, so to speak. As a matter of fact, you were doing duty down in South Nam and the Southern Command and, I think, doing some excellent work.

But one of the things that I tried to do, after the trip, after my discussion with people like the President of Peru and folks that we have on the ground in Bolivia and our folks in DEA and other intelligence areas in Colombia and working with people in—talking to people in Panama, and then also the Government of Mexico, I really started to understand the real frustrations, that this isn't an easy process, it's a process that's pockmarked with politics, international politics as well as internal politics.

And one of the things, when you talked to me, being able to go out and bolster the appropriation process, the job that the Speaker asked me to do, I took a lot of your information. I think in most cases we were pretty successful.

But one of the frustrations I had, when I went to a subcommittee chairman on Appropriations, he sanctimoniously waved the RAND study in my face and says, well, you guys are all wrong about interdiction. It doesn't make any difference at all. We need to put the money some place else, so we are going to gut the Coast Guard. That was wrong.

I was looking for something, and I guess sometimes we all look for something to bolster our views on what is right and what is wrong, to counter the RAND study, quite frankly. When I saw this, I was interested—most interested.

Would you give the general a copy of this? This was something that was just handed out, something I looked at before. The people that wrote this weren't economists. The gentleman who wrote this——

General MCCAFFREY. Like you and I.

Mr. HASTERT. What?

General MCCAFFREY. They were not economists like you and I.

Mr. HASTERT. Were not economists, was not an economist, did not have the degrees that you or I might have in economics.

But the gentleman is known as a physicist, and I guess a physicist looks at cause and effect and tree—apples falling out of trees and things like that. This shows cause and effect, and it's very striking, I think.

General MCCAFFREY. See, I wouldn't agree that it shows cause and effect at all. This shows correlation. That's different.

Mr. HASTERT. Let's agree that we don't disagree.

General MCCAFFREY. But I mean, it's important to understand that, you know, that there's a—it's just like the relationship between smoking marijuana and cocaine addiction. There's a tremendous statistical correlation but no necessary causal relationship.

Mr. HASTERT. Anyway, what happened in this is that price went up and purity—price went down and purity went up, you know, and the whole correlation in that. So if you want to use the word "correlation," it happened. Now, that's significant.

But the real concern that I have—and the record of the predecessor that you had was quite different from when I sat on this panel in this committee 10 years ago and worked with Admiral Yost in the Coast Guard and worked with a drug czar under another administration that made a difference. I mean, those efforts really started to choke down—you were a part of that—choke down—they were successful in interdiction and did start to drive down the use of drugs in this country.

One of the reasons, I think—I don't have any empirical evidence to show that, but drug abuse was cut down during those early—late years in the eighties and early years in the nineties. And all of a sudden, when there was $500 million that were transferred out of interdiction, before you ever became—had the job you did, and it was supposed to be a real shift between interdiction in source country, and the shift never happened, those dollars never went in. We then saw the results of a huge increase in drug use, especially among teenagers.

General MCCAFFREY. Now, to be fair though, sir, there has not been a huge increase in drug use, nor did any of these drive up the seizure rates of cocaine over the years.

See, that's the problem. The increase among teenage drug use, which is almost completely marijuana and other products, not cocaine, not heroin, did not respond to any of this interdiction effort. I say that just as a scientific observer and a participant in the process.

Mr. HASTERT. Well, our sources say there was heroin and heroin is coming back. But the other part of it was——

General MCCAFFREY. Right.

Mr. HASTERT [continuing]. That the statement on heroin was that people were using needles.

General MCCAFFREY. No; I agree. I just meant that chart on cocaine, we got almost the same amount year after year. That's frustrating to those of us who were working the interdiction community, and we are going to work it smarter in the next several years. But year after year, we got—the cocaine coming into America stayed about the same, and thank God the number of people using it dropped dramatically, 75 percent in the last 15 years.

They are sticking about 300 tons up their nose still, or using crack products. We didn't affect drug abuse in America through the interdiction campaign. That doesn't mean it wasn't a tremendously valuable effort.

Mr. HASTERT. Well, I mean, we have evidence—we can talk about evidence and empirical evidence going back and forth, but there are things that show that in 1993 drug abuse did start to go up; emergency rooms did take in more.

General MCCAFFREY. Emergency rooms doesn't relate to drug use.

Mr. HASTERT. It does when you start to take kids who are—use drugs and are OD because the purity of drugs is a lot higher than they thought it was.

So I don't want to argue back and forth. My point is that, from this point forward, we need to work together.

General MCCAFFREY. Yes.

Mr. HASTERT. I think many of us have taken a good first step. I worked diligently to make sure that your requests, a kind of a unique situation that I had, were filled, and that, in fact, you have another $60 million at your discretion, because I think you need some money at your discretion.

I would certainly be interested, as soon as you have been able to swallow everything and digest it, where that money is going to go and how you think that discretionary fund should be spent.

So there is, in my view, cause and effect. I think we need to put our money in good causes. We need to spend it intelligently. As a matter of fact, when we use that word, sometimes I think maybe intelligence, there's not enough intelligence, and the more money we put in intelligence, to know where that money—where that product comes from, how it's moved through the channel and being able to intercept it is tied to intelligence. We probably don't put enough emphasis on that.

General MCCAFFREY. I agree.

Mr. HASTERT. And how we can best set up a strategy so when that we come into 1998—and I understand you were caught in the switches of the 1997 budget, and I sympathize with the situation. You came in, a lot of transition going on, and the House and, in some cases, the Senate, they had already put their appropriations to bed before you ever got a chance to get involved. We have turned that around. I think you have gotten everything—almost everything that you have needed to do, including your staff, that you needed to do.

Now, we want to see how best we can fight this. I think interdiction is a very important part of this thing.

General MCCAFFREY. I agree.

Mr. HASTERT. I think source country is a very important part of this. Now, I may be proved wrong, and we can throw statistics around to prove it. I think this is a starting point that we need to work together. I think it's unfortunate that this happens, a misunderstanding of what you said, what the feelings are and why things were suppressed or why things weren't suppressed. But I think from this point on, we need to work together. I think we need to get serious about doing that. And I can tell you, as long as I am around here, and I can affect some of this legislation, I am there to bat for you.

General MCCAFFREY. Yes, sir.

Mr. HASTERT. We have got to have the right information. We have got to be able to listen to all things and hopefully build upon what knowledge we have.

And I have always been uncomfortable with the RAND situation because, as you said, you can put all kinds of economic models together, but models don't always tell what the effects are properly. And to rely on one study, which really makes policy, has driven the policy of the previous drug czar, to say that's right and something else doesn't belong in the mix, I think, is wrong. I hope we can work together to rectify that.

General MCCAFFREY. I would welcome that.

Mr. ZELIFF. If the gentleman would yield for just a quick minute?

Mr. HASTERT. Yes.

Mr. ZELIFF. For the last 2 years, long before you arrived on the scene, we have been critical on this subcommittee of the lack of interdiction efforts, the major cuts in interdiction, the major cuts in source-country programs. We came back—after going down and taking a look at it firsthand, we were then totally convinced that the policy was wrong. We came back and tried to influence changes with you, but I think the strategy was already set. And that's no fault of yours. It was moving before you even got there.

In spite of that, we gave you the resources. We fought like the devil to make sure that your office was funded, you will remember that, so that you could start putting together the right policies.

So I would like to say to you, this subcommittee here is greatly concerned about the fact that we are using bad data, RAND data, to drive the treatment—the $2.9 billion, I believe, of treatment moneys that we now have in the 1997 appropriations bill, and we were fighting to patch up and boost up moneys for the Coast Guard in other areas.

Let me just ask you this question: You know, are we on the right track? Are you in agreement? Are you willing to sit down with this subcommittee?

Are we willing to start—if IDA doesn't work, then what other information is out there? You know, we don't want to reject information for the sake of rejecting it, but maybe we need to get information that people believe in. Maybe we ought to check with an independent source whether IDA knows what they are talking about.

But the bottom line here is that we have got kids dying on the streets and we need to somehow figure out what is the right balance. And again, it's a five-legged stool; it's education, prevention, treatment, interdiction, and source-country programs. If you pull one leg of the stool, then the stool caves in.

Comments?

General MCCAFFREY. Well, I think the way you put that concept together, I support what you said. You talked about the balanced strategy. I couldn't agree more.

The one caution I would add, sir, if I may, is that my criticism of the RAND Corp. study's impact on policy analysis did not mean to imply that I don't absolutely believe that we must provide effective treatment programs for those who are addicted. If we want to stop crime and violence in America, we have got to do things like break the cycle, the drug courts.

We have got to go to Baltimore, Miami, rural Iowa, San Diego, and get those who are addicted, the 2.1 million Americans who consume 80 percent of the drugs in America, and two-thirds of them are involved in the criminal justice system in a given year, we simply must pay the costs to provide drug treatment and follow-on care. As a taxpayer, it makes sense.

Mr. ZELIFF. But we have to also look at the effectiveness of those drug treatment programs.

General MCCAFFREY. Absolutely. I agree.

Mr. ZELIFF. So far, we are not seeming to make a dent in it, despite the fact that we have invested major resources.

Mr. HASTERT. Will the gentleman yield back?

Mr. ZELIFF. And the chart is right here on page 15.

Mr. HASTERT. Just very briefly though, on that statement that you make, I think you have to treat those people who are drug addicts and who are hooked, but we need to be able to take that marginal stuff off the street, where a kid wants to experiment, and it's cheap, and it's there, and why not try it?

General MCCAFFREY. Absolutely.

Mr. HASTERT. If we could remove that—because those are the kids in my district, in Aurora, IL, and Elgin, IL. We have some of the biggest drug kingpins right there. It is close to Chicago, and the heat is not out there. And in Northern Illinois University, De Kalb, kids who can be delivered easy from Chicago or Aurora or Elgin, and they are the ones who are experimenting, and if it's there, and it's cheap and it's available, they are the ones who are experimental, recreational users, if you will, if that's such a thing. But they get hooked. Let's stop that from happening.

General MCCAFFREY. Mr. Hastert, you are exactly right. That's why interdiction, whether or not it changes the price or the purity, is so vital to America, because if we take 100 tons out of the school systems and the cities, less kids are going to fool around with drugs. And there's an algorithm there, known but to God, in which some number get addicted.

So I couldn't agree with your point more. I think you are entirely correct. That's law enforcement as well as interdiction.

Mr. ZELIFF. I am going to throw in one quick comment, because I was trying to finish this. But if you look at this chart here, this is the number of people being treated. It is going down. This is the number—the costs, inflation adjusted, of the moneys and resources going into treatment. So the amount of money that we put into treatment is not necessarily working, and so that's got to be looked at as well.

General MCCAFFREY. Yes, sir.

Mr. ZELIFF. Mr. Mica from Florida.

Mr. MICA. General, you have been involved in this drug war for some time, and I, too, have been involved in it. I came as a staffer in the Senate in 1980, with Senator Hawkins, when our State, Florida, was ravaged by a drug war on our streets, literally.

As a staffer, I helped write some of the legislation that we work under now, the certification language I drafted that came up with putting some of the resources into interdiction in source countries, trying to make sure that we approach this problem from an education, treatment, interdiction, and enforcement standpoint.

When I came to Congress, I was still concerned about it, and not many people were talking about it in 1992 or 1993, and I will be glad to get the record and show you the statements I made trying to get even one hearing in this committee.

And when you were—well, your predecessor, I wasn't very pleased with his performance or the administration's policy, because it didn't take much—I don't have a science degree, I am not an economist or whatever background you have, but——

General MCCAFFREY. Sir, could you pull that microphone over? I am having trouble.

Mr. MICA. I looked at the results, and when you see that we cut interdiction through the RAND study, or through whatever study, we put our resources on treatment, sort of treating just the wounded in the battle, a tremendous emphasis on that and away from some of the other emphasis that I felt were necessary, including some in transit zone and even more in source countries, and they weren't done under the last Congress or under this administration.

Then I think when you were appointed, I was one of the first to offer my assistance on this panel to get you whatever resources.

We went to South America. Some of us spent time away from our families. It was not one of these trips where everybody takes their spouse along. We went into the jungles. We talked to DEA agents on the ground. We tried to learn what was happening, and then we came back.

We got the Speaker to provide some leadership. Mr. Hastert joined us, and it became a project of this new Congress.

I am telling you that because then, in working the last few weeks to get the legislation through, to put the funds in here, to restore these things that had been cut out, and some of the emphasis that had been cut out, I heard from people around you that there was a report that wasn't coming out. I heard that the report had been presented some time ago and wasn't coming out and was getting, for lack of a better term, buried. I wasn't a happy person.

I asked you about some of those questions I had, and I felt this deserved a hearing because this is a critical report. And even today, you said, "I don't agree with this study yet," I think was your comment just a few minutes ago. I tried to take it down.

Well, we are trying to make decisions at a time when there are very limited resources here. We are up to hock to our eyeballs, and we are trying to decide between programs of importance to the country, without driving it further into debt. So our purpose is to get the best information, for you to share that information with us, and that we have that in a timely fashion to make those decisions on behalf of the citizens we represent.

You could almost predict the headlines that I held up here today, basically because we have stopped interdiction, because we stopped some of the source-country programs, because we haven't put a proper emphasis on all of the areas necessary.

Also, most importantly, we haven't provided the leadership from the White House. Your predecessor didn't provide the leadership. The highest chief health officer of this country didn't provide the leadership and made a joke out of legalization. And I submit even the President, in his statements on MTV and saying that he would have inhaled if he had it to do over again, doesn't meet goal 1: Motivate America's youth to reject illegal drugs and substance abuse.

So that's my comment.

My question—and I am not going to get into who said what to whom; some of that has been charged already. My question is: Do you believe that we can work together, that we can find some solutions, that your office can be open with this committee and our subcommittee and see if we can't work together just to put our limited resources most effectively where they can do the best job?

General MCCAFFREY. I would welcome that opportunity. I would indeed.

Mr. MICA. Finally, I think it's important that as we develop this drug strategy and also direct the limited resources of this Congress and the American people, we do it in the most effective manner.

Do you have further recommendations, and in what order of sequence will they be provided to this Congress and the subcommittee so we can pick up from where we have left off in providing you the assets that you need to do the job?

General MCCAFFREY. Mr. Congressman, I need to write an intelligent 1998 budget request in full cooperation with the 14 other Cabinet officers who were involved in this. That is step No. 1. Then I need to devise a 5-year budget concept, then submit it to the President, the Cabinet, and get it down here and see what you all think about it.

If I don't do that, we will never break out of the kind of exchanges we are now having, and that is what I dedicate myself to doing between now and next summer.

Mr. MICA. I thank you. And I think my time has expired.

General MCCAFFREY. Mr. Chairman, I should—as you know, the 1998 law establishing my position states that I am a political officer. I have been a soldier since I was 17 years old. I took this job, and I am honored to be part of it.

And having said that, you should be aware that I have been working with this President for the last 3 years and with the team of Janet Reno, Donna Shalala, Bill Perry, the CIA, and others, and Admiral Kramek, and Tom Constantine, and Louis Freeh. And you should understand, and I don't say this in rebuttal to Mr. Mica, but merely to put on the table my absolute respect for their cooperative leadership and my belief that they are committed to a nondrug, nonstoned America.

Mr. ZELIFF. General, I can appreciate that, and I certainly would agree to some degree. I am just concerned—we are concerned about some information here that's been under oath that is a bit in conflict, and we are going to have to discuss that.

And I think the other piece that I would just—there is a letter apparently written in the Wall Street Journal. There was a letter from Administrator Louis Freeh from the FBI and Tom Constantine, who also, both of those gentlemen I have tremendous respect for, talking about a National Drug Strategy adrift.

Are you aware of that letter, and could you kind of describe what the contents of that letter would be?

General MCCAFFREY. I have no knowledge at all about the letter except what I read in the press, the scuttlebutt.

Mr. ZELIFF. We have asked the President for a copy of it, and we have been told that he wrote Executive privilege.

General MCCAFFREY. It is not part of my watch, and I don't have any involvement in it.

Mr. ZELIFF. Relative to the degree of what is happening in the drug war today in America, I would just like to read to you from some of the testimony we have had in our previous hearings, and this relates to drug emergencies at record level.

As indicated earlier, another critical negative impact of drugs is, alarming new data on drug-related emergencies, increasing drug-related medical emergencies, first became obvious in 1993 when the Drug Abuse Warning Network, DAWN, collected data from emergency rooms around the country and released it in December 1994. That data showed an 8 percent increase in drug-related emergency cases between 1992 and 1993, with 45 percent being heroin overdoses. It is not just marijuana. Cocaine was also at an all-time high, having more than doubled since 1988. Marijuana emergencies increased 22 percent between 1992 and 1993.

On top of this, marijuana- or hashish-related emergencies rose 39 percent from 1993 to 1994, and total drug-related emergency cases rose 10 percent between 1993 and 1994. Heroin-related emergencies increased between 1994 and 1995 by 19 percent. We believe very strongly that we have an epidemic and a crisis.

Would you care to comment?

General MCCAFFREY. Quite clearly, in particular, heroin, with its very high purity and increasing availability, worldwide production having doubled in the last 10 years, it is going to represent a very fundamental threat to our population.

The data to which you refer, though, to put it in context, are, in general, driven by aging cohorts of addicts, and when they get sick, they come in off the streets to emergency rooms. That is not completely true, because there is an increase among youngsters also and new heroin users, but, in general, that is the 30-year-old to 40-year-old who is now dying because he is using, he or she is using, crack or heroin. That is who is coming in the hospitals.

Mr. ZELIFF. One last quick question here. You are familiar, I believe, with the April 11, 1996 letter from Mr. Boyer, and this is to Dr. Barry Crane. And just two comments.

The draft paper on source-zone interdiction effectiveness is an excellent step toward quantifying this. It is gratifying to see that the impact can be quantified.

Then on the second page: Recommend deleting or softening any language that appears to be either combative with or condescending to the RAND study or IDA. Instead, take a positive approach toward source-zone efforts and let the IDA speak for itself.

Then last, the discussion of the cost-effectiveness of treatment programs is a great value but not necessary to the interdiction programs and possibly beyond the purview of USIC. IDA recommends this issue be removed from the paper and treated separately in an appendix. And then, written on the bottom, "good work."

What I am hearing you say is that you don't believe it is good work and that you disagree with any or most of the findings.

General McCAFFREY. What you said was, you talked about, I read Boyer's memo, I read through it in the last 2 or 3 days. It is a pretty balanced memo. It lays out his concerns about the study.

I think he correctly, to be honest, made the point that in their analysis they wanted to support interdiction as having value to the U.S. Drug Strategy, and don't contaminate it by going after the RAND study, and don't talk about its contributions in the interdiction's campaign to what I think is a dubious proposition, that interdiction, in the short run, would drive up costs, drive down use.

I don't believe it. That is not what we are seeing on the streets. And since I like the IDA attempt, they ought to focus, in my view—I haven't told them this; I am not telling them this—they ought to focus on why your dollars that you are giving me this year for interdiction payoff.

They ought to go find the payoffs, and it will be there. It will be there in the increased retail costs. We are seeing thousands of campesinos leave the coca fields in Peru and head into Lima. There are payoffs to interdiction.

I just personally think it is nonsense to say I am going to go down to Baltimore and find the crack prices are up and use is down. If we get better interdiction and we start taking away two-thirds of it instead of a third of it, I would suspect my conclusions are incorrect. They are welcome to study anything they want.

Mr. ZELIFF. My hope would be that if someone comes to see me and has some answers on interdiction, I think we all have to be willing to have an open mind, and I believe you said that you would.

Just one last comment that is really troubling me. I have gotten back from the recorder here—do you have a copy of the cable?

I believe Dr. Rivolo had indicated that going back, or I guess while he was there, Admiral Kramek came out and told him certain things: That this was not to see the light of the day. And in the staff vehicle on the ride back to the Pentagon, it was his understanding that, until further notice, none of this was to get out.

My problem here is that they have apparently gone from a meeting and have come back with some rather dramatic differences of opinion as to what happened. You have been pretty direct. But, again, would you refer to this one statement from the recorder; and second, who was in the room? Was it Captain Boyer and Admiral Kramek, General McCaffrey? And did General McCaffrey go out to meet with those folks, or is it all part of their imagination?

I guess that is the concern that I have here as I leave this room, that we haven't resolved apparently a major controversy of who heard what, and I think it only has to do with, are we willing to have an open mind, and are we willing to move forward?

General McCAFFREY. Of course, I am not a politician. I am a soldier now serving the Drug Policy Office. I am sympathetic to these people leaving—I didn't go out and talk to them. They didn't brief me. They are good people. They come from a reputable institute. They are going to have a study that contributes to the understanding of the problem, but they probably left disappointed.

I didn't like the study. I thought it was incorrect. I am an expert on drug interdiction, but at some point their study will help form our thinking, and I absolutely commit myself to several viewpoints and welcoming the direct involvement of Congress in this process.

Mr. ZELIFF. I think at this point we—I would like to say what others have said in the past, you are our great hope. I have said that to you directly, and I have said it to you publicly. I have made a major commitment. I am leaving Congress, but I came back today for this hearing. I am totally committed to what we are trying to do.

It goes way beyond personalities. No one single person has all of the answers, and I think you would be the first to admit that. While we have great respect for you, we are going to do everything we can to make sure we are on track and that we don't allow politics to derail this effort, because if we do, then you are getting into my grandchildren and kids, and I, like my good friend from Baltimore, I don't think we are going to allow it to happen.

Again, you are our great hope, and we are there. We have shown as recently as in the last 3 days—strategic resources that you need to do your job, but we have to somehow be willing to open up and be willing to take information as it comes along, and reverse strategies if we have to do that, and let the chips fall where they may.

Mr. Mica.

Mr. MICA. Mr. Chairman, since you opened this up, just one last question for the general for the record.

General, did you——

Mr. ZELIFF. I didn't open up for more questions. If you would like to make a statement, that is pretty fair.

Mr. MICA. I just wonder if the general could respond if he did, in fact, say to Admiral Kramek or to anyone else, that not a word of this report is to get out?

General MCCAFFREY. No. And, in fact, I sent the report out all over the country for review by scientific——

Mr. MICA. That was sometime later.

General MCCAFFREY. No, I don't think so.

Mr. MICA. You did not say to anyone, "Not a word of this to anyone"——

General MCCAFFREY. No.

Mr. ZELIFF. OK.

Mr. Cummings.

Mr. CUMMINGS. Just a brief statement, general.

I guess you already know this, but you have, in my opinion, the most important job in this country. I just want to take a moment to thank you. I have not known you long, but I am very, very impressed. Your integrity speaks volumes. And I just want to encourage you to stay on your path. As a matter of fact, the very budget that this committee has supported you shows that we do support you and what you are trying to do.

Finally, let me say this, that the thing I guess I like about what you are trying to do is, you are trying to hit this problem from several different areas. And I believe very strongly in interdiction, I really do, but I also believe very strongly in people who are addicted and trying to make them well.

We have got—my office has gotten hundreds of calls over the course of this hearing saying, just speak up for us, we are trying to get well, so we don't have to—so there won't be a problem, so for them, for all of them. I speak for them, and I thank you for taking them into consideration so they can get better. We only have one life to live, and I guess that is, this is it. So I really appreciate it for them.

Mr. ZELIFF. OK.

Mr. Cummings, Mr. Mica, Mr. Hastert, Mr. Clinger, and on behalf of myself, general, thank you very much. We appreciate very much your testimony here today, and we wish you good luck in what is a very tough assignment, probably the toughest in the United States.

I ask unanimous consent to submit all questions into the record.

Without objection, so ordered.

We will move to the next panel.

I would like to welcome Adm. Robert Kramek, the Commandant of the U.S. Coast Guard, U.S. Interdiction Coordinator.

We appreciate your patience. It has been a rather long 2 or 3 hours, I believe.

If you would stand and raise your right hand.

[Witness sworn.]

Mr. ZELIFF. If you could summarize perhaps your statement, and we will obviously accept it.

STATEMENT OF ADM. ROBERT E. KRAMEK, COMMANDANT, U.S. COAST GUARD, U.S. INTERDICTION COORDINATOR

Admiral KRAMEK. Thank you, Mr. Chairman and distinguished members of the subcommittee. I certainly welcome the opportunity to discuss our interdiction program and any questions you might have concerning the report by the Institute for Defense Analysis.

As Interdiction Coordinator, my responsibility is oversight and coordination of interdiction efforts in the Western Hemisphere. I have been involved with these counternarcotics operations for over 21 years.

When I first started in 1975, I was on a Coast Guard cutter, *Galveston,* conducting Operation Buccaneer in the Caribbean and the Bahamas. Much has changed in the last 21 years. Blatant landings of marijuana and cocaine on our shores are not an everyday event.

In 1990 to 1992, I lead the effort in the transit zone, not only for the Coast Guard, but at that time I was both Dr. Bennett's Interdiction Coordinator in the area and then Governor Martinez, two previous Drug Czars before General McCaffrey. In 1994, I was appointed by the President to be the Interdiction Coordinator, then report to the third Drug Czar, Dr. Brown. I am very honored now to be able to serve General McCaffrey in the same capacity.

Also in 1994, Presidential Decision Directive 14 was promulgated which did a number of things that are pertinent to our discussion today.

First, they appointed me as the Interdiction Coordinator, and "coordinate" was the word used, not in command and control of all the operations, but to coordinate the entire effort interdicting drugs into the Western Hemisphere up to our shoreline.

I was also to see if all of the agencies involved in this endeavor to carry out the strategy at that time had sufficient resources to do the job.

I was also tasked with making sure that they were deploying the resources they had properly and in the most efficient manner.

And my fourth major task was to see if the strategy was working and, if it wasn't, to recommend any changes to that strategy.

I have done all four of those things for the last 2 years. As you know, I have stood before this committee on one occasion before and met with you on many occasions.

I am delighted now that we have a 1996 strategy. I am also delighted that I was able to get all of the commanders and all the agencies responsible for this effort that I described to you together on at least five occasions in the last 2 years and get all of their requirements for what needs to be done to make our strategy work.

The results of those requirements have been incorporated in the 1996 Strategy and were incorporated in the President's supplemental budget to Congress in April 1996, this year, requesting resources of about $250 million to further progress our interests, mostly in the interdiction efforts.

I know it has been a long history of funding. I am delighted this weekend that it appears that in the omnibus appropriations bill that closed out this session of Congress, that much of those funds have been provided.

My staff is still analyzing all of that to determine exactly in what pot the moneys were provided, but it certainly looks like most of the things that the President has asked the Congress for in support of the 1996 strategy, as presented by General McCaffrey, will now be provided commencing today, October 1. This is very, very important, because right now there are major operations under way.

The newest one, which commenced this morning, is to close off all drug routes to and from Puerto Rico and the Virgin Islands, this operation, called Frontier Shield, commenced at 10 a.m. this morning. Also, Laser Strike is under way, as you know, and Operation Gateway by Customs. Steel Web is planned, and other major operations, anticipating that those funds would be provided and also carried through next year in next year's budget.

I think that over the last 2 years the administration has greatly changed its policy in putting together the 1996 strategy and has moved in a direction that has been greatly assisted by the findings of this particular committee as well as Senator Hatch's committee in the Senate, on bringing the drug problem to a great national debate again and making sure that we attack the problem.

Now, I will say that there is no panacea, no silver bullet. We all know that. The source-nation strategy, for example, is not the complete answer to interdiction, and interdiction is not the complete answer to drug control. Our control strategy provides a balanced approach, as General McCaffrey presented it.

As Interdiction Coordinator, I was cautiously optimistic about the preliminary findings of the IDA report. My staff reviewed the first draft of this study in April. They identified some problem areas. They communicated those to the contractors in a letter which has been sent to you in your request for information. Others I see have made similar comments, and although I haven't seen them all, I am told IDA has produced additional drafts. The draft I commented on at that time was draft No. 2.

I considered at that time for it to be a work in progress. I did brief, in May, General McCaffrey on that particular work in progress. I took IDA with me to that briefing in hopes that they may be able to give a full briefing. The briefing that I gave was sufficient for the drug czar at that time, and it was a work in progress. It had not been vetted by peer review. Previous to that, I had taken it to the Interdiction Committee; TIC is the acronym for that.

TIC advises me as the U.S. Interdiction Coordinator. It consists of the Commissioner of Customs, the Administrator of DEA, the Bureau of Narcotics and Law Enforcement, the J–3 at the Pentagon on the Joint Staff, the Head of the Border Patrol at INS, and others as well. This review was given to TIC almost 2 months ago, and that was based on draft No. 1. They advised that the data was insufficient, it needed peer review, it needed more data points, and we needed to tell IDA to continue on with their study, which is what we did.

I would also like to tell you that before I answer any questions that you may have, that IDA does a lot for the U.S. Interdiction Coordinator which has not been reported here. This particular report in question is one small piece of their work. Most of their work is classified.

Barry Crane and others have probably told you that recently they have been to Panama and all over the place. What they do for me is, they provide me with information on where the smugglers are going, where the maritime tracks are, where the air tracks are, what is happening in the air bridge, hundreds and hundreds and hundreds of pieces of information of tracking data.

The commanders use that information, which is all classified, it is all based on intelligence, it is all based on sensor information, to determine where we should put our emphasis on interdiction, and that has been very, very successful.

All of their data is immediately turned over to the commanders and used—and it is probably one of the most successful things and pieces of intelligence we have used for interdiction in the last 5 or 6 years.

I would be delighted at future hearings in closed session, because it is all classified, to show you how we use the predominance of data that is provided almost on a weekly basis by IDA.

Mr. Chairman, that concludes my oral statement, and I would be very happy to answer any questions that you have at this time.

Mr. ZELIFF. Thank you, admiral.

[The prepared statement of Admiral Kramek follows:]

Good morning, Mr. Chairman and distinguished members of the subcommittee. I welcome the opportunity to discuss our interdiction program and the study being conducted by the Institute for Defense Analyses, entitled "An Empirical Examination of Counterdrug Interdiction Program Effectiveness."

As U. S. Interdiction Coordinator, my responsibility is oversight and coordination of interdiction efforts in the Western Hemisphere. From that perspective, I am keenly interested in any analysis of the effectiveness of interdiction programs and will limit my comments to this area. I believe that our counterdrug program must be a balanced approach, including strong components of prevention, treatment, law enforcement, interdiction, and international programs. The loss of appropriate emphasis on any one of these components would seriously impact our overall effort. Our National Drug Control Strategy represents this kind of a comprehensive approach and interdiction is a single, vital component of the whole.

We have come a long way from the days of the mid-eighties when drug traffickers delivered their cargo directly to the beaches of Florida, and escalating drug-related violence forced the problem into national prominence. But there is still much ground to cover. I would like to briefly talk about how our approach to protecting our borders from the scourge of illegal drugs has evolved over the years and how it must continue to evolve to counter the ever-changing threat.

Interdiction successes have forced drug traffickers to change their routes and become more sophisticated in their operations, increasing both their transportation costs and their risk of apprehension. Traffickers once were able to fly their drugs directly from Colombia to small islands in the Bahamas and then on to air drop sites in Florida and our coastal waters. In response we developed interdiction capabilities in the Caribbean. Through the combined efforts of the Coast Guard, Customs, DEA, DOD, and cooperating governments in the Caribbean, we have forced narco-trafficking aircraft away from the direct Central Caribbean approach to the United States. As a result of this success we have seen a shift in trafficker patterns. The new challenge comes from traffickers who approach the United States indirectly through the Eastern Caribbean, the Mexico/Central America corridor, and the Eastern Pacific; or by hiding their drugs in commercial cargo shipments. Most recently we have even seen the desperate measure of an attempted non-stop drug flight from Colombia to Canada. Through the combined and coordinated efforts of U. S. and Canadian agencies that flight ended in the seizure of 510 kilos of cocaine, one aircraft, three vehicles, two boats, and the arrest of six drug smugglers.

We must maintain pressure on drug shipping routes to reduce the supply of drugs in our country and signal our political will. In 1994 we began a shift of emphasis among interdiction priorities from the transit zone to the source countries where drugs are produced. At this moment there are over 300 U. S. military and law enforcement personnel deployed to South America participating in Operation Laser Strike, supporting our allies with counterdrug training, intelligence collection, and sophisticated detection and monitoring equipment. The benefits of this presence can be seen in the destruction of cocaine labs, the seizure of drugs ready for smuggling, as well as the chemicals used to produce them, the eradication of coca crops, and in the arrest of drug cartel leaders.

Our source country strategy is starting to work but it is not a panacea. We must and will maintain pressure on established transit routes and on new routes as they emerge. To increase the cost-effectiveness of transit zone interdiction we have increased our reliance on intelligence cueing. This allows us to conserve resources by focusing on known or probable smuggling events. The interdiction process is much more efficient when we can focus on a specific flight, a specific fishing boat, or a specific shipping container. As we apply pressure on established smuggling routes new routes will emerge and smugglers will attempt to reopen old routes. Here again, effective intelligence will help us to stay one step ahead of the challenge.

I must stress again that just as our source nation strategy is not the complete answer to interdiction, interdiction is not the complete answer to drug control. Our National Drug Control Strategy provides a multi-pronged, balanced approach that will reduce the demand for and supply of illegal drugs. When there is no longer a demand for illegal drugs it will no longer be profitable to smuggle them across our borders. The reduction of demand is a long term process that must be given time to become effective. While this process unfolds we must continue to shield our borders and send an unmistakable signal of our determination through a robust and flexible program of interdiction.

As the Interdiction Coordinator I am made cautiously optimistic by the preliminary findings of the IDA report which show that historically, specific major interdiction events have been closely correlated to shifts in domestic drug prices, diminished drug purity, and decreased drug use in the United States. At the same time, however, I feel we must subject IDA's findings to the same critical review that any other scientific report would receive prior to acceptance. My staff reviewed the first draft of this study in April. They identified some problem areas, and they communicated those to the contractor. Others have made similar comments, and, although I haven't seen them, I am told that IDA has produced additional drafts that have refined the research. I consider this to be a work in progress, and I look forward to seeing the results of the final product.

Mr. Chairman, this concludes my prepared remarks. Thank you for the opportunity to appear before this distinguished committee. I would be happy to answer any questions you may have.

45-081 98 - 5

Mr. ZELIFF. I would like to start out by saying that I have a great deal of respect for you and the uniform you wear, and I think you are probably one the finest people in our military. I don't pass that on lightly, but I appreciate the hard work that you do, and you have been very responsive to this subcommittee.

I think you can understand why we are a little concerned when we have conflicting testimony under oath. It is not a big deal if we can just kind of solve it and talk about interdiction, talk about some of the other great things that you are doing, things that you initiated today. But it does bother me a lot when we have people like IDA, that are well-respected within the Pentagon, that do studies for you and others, and we can't seem to get whatever really happened there out.

This is a report that took 18 months to develop. It has now taken 7 months since then, and is still not final. I can't believe the process that we go through when we keep sending it back and changing it, and, you know, according to, I guess, the way you want it to come out.

I don't know, but you have heard the testimony we had this morning, and for a person who basically comes from the business community like me, you wonder if we are getting good bang for our buck. By the time it gets revised and gets out, how useful can the information be?

And, frankly, our big concern here is that, were we gypped out of a resource? In putting the 1997 funding strategy together, are we going down the same old road, or are we willing to listen and open up our minds to the fact that there are some changes?

I know you are, but what is very discouraging, frankly, is that people swore under oath that, you know, they went to a briefing that never occurred. You, in turn, were asked to do the briefing, and then you came out and had to apologize, according to their words, for the fact that they weren't going to be briefing General McCaffrey. You appeared to be—this is not my words, it is their words—upset in the process of explaining to them that the briefing wasn't going to take place; and the fact you also said this was not to see the light of day.

I don't know whether—what motivation they have for lying, or whether they did, in fact, lie, or maybe they misinterpreted your comments. Maybe you can clarify that a little bit for us.

Admiral KRAMEK. I would be delighted to.

I have been in the forces for 39 years. I don't ever recall lying, and I certainly would not enjoy being accused of ever doing that.

Mr. ZELIFF. I hope you don't take this—I am not accusing anybody, I am just trying to settle with—putting it together.

Admiral KRAMEK. I think I can clarify a lot of this for you. I was there. I was in the briefing. I was the one that told IDA not to give the briefing the next day. I can explain all of that to you and why that was so.

First of all, IDA had been providing very useful data for me. As you said, the Department of Defense had the funds for that, but I am to coordinate all of these 32 different agencies.

This report was not information we would normally use. I use track data. I use the intelligence data. I put down all of their tracks and look at that and say, we know what to do about that, we know how to shut those tracks down, we know how to stop the supply of coca. That was Green Clover, now Operation Laser Strike.

This report that they put together first came to my attention because they gave me an oral brief of data that they were finding on major operations that, in their opinion, had caused an effect on price, impurity, and demand in December, and they said they would be ready to make a better presentation in January. And on January 11, IDA—January 11, 1996, IDA gave me a brief that showed some of the graphs that are in the current version of their report, some very similar to that. That was very, very dramatic data.

My entire USIC staff consists of five people. I don't have any analysts or any assistants that could analyze that, but I have a very, very experienced committee, the Interdiction Committee, TIC, that I explained to you before, which advised me, and I called the first and only emergency meeting of TIC that I ever knew of. They responded and, on January 17, met in my briefing room in Coast Guard headquarters, where I presented the IDA report and all of those charts to TIC.

Their total consensus of opinion was, the data was preliminary. There were lots of questions by DEA that really reflected what was going on. There were only a couple of data points on Operation Green Clover, which had terminated on December 15, just 1 month before.

We were anxious to get on and go to sustained operations to see if, in fact, this data would continue to show the trends that IDA predicted, and the Department of Defense representatives who contracted for the report had not given it any review. This was preliminary data, preliminary information.

Mr. ZELIFF. Did you ever say at the end of this meeting, "Not a word of this was to get out"?

Admiral KRAMEK. That was in January. In April, I was given draft No. 2 on April 4. I then made a written comment to Gary Boyer, my executive director, we provided you that information, made a written critique of that particular report that IDA put together.

The next month, I held a U.S. Interdiction Coordinator Joint Staff planning conference at the Pentagon where all the commanders came into town. On the first day of that conference, IDA briefed that report to all the commanders. That was the same day that I briefed—that was the morning. In the afternoon, it was my first briefing to the new drug czar.

Once every other month, I sit down with General McCaffrey and give him a briefing status report of everything that is going on in the interdiction community. As part of that briefing, one item of perhaps eight or nine that I briefed him on was the status of the IDA report. I told him I had the analysts out in his outer lobby if he had the time to receive the full report. He said, will you brief me now, tell me what this report is about? I gave him a quick briefing. He said, does it have peer review? I said no. I told him that I had vetted the same briefing through the interdiction committee. They had the exact same opinion of the report as he did. He said it needed peer review, we needed to have peer review, and he didn't want to receive the full report until it was a final report delivered to the sponsoring Department of Defense and it had gotten proper peer review.

I then left and went out into the hallway. On the way out, I told Barry Crane, I am very sorry you won't be able to present this today, it is preliminary, it is not ready for prime time, I think I told him, and it needs to be reviewed.

Mr. ZELIFF. Did you or did you not say that not a word of this was to get out?

Admiral KRAMEK. No; what I told him was the USIC commanders conference that I hold on a quarterly basis is always a 2-day meeting. First day, the working groups meet together, and the second day, the principals meet.

Barry Crane's group had already presented this information to the working group. I told him I did not want the conclusions of the report presented to the principals the next day because it was preliminary, it wasn't approved, TIC didn't agree with it, the drug czar didn't agree with the draft, and it hadn't had peer review. He could present all the data, he would present the curves, he would present the information, but he wasn't to present any of the conclusions and comments about other studies in other reports because it hadn't been vetted, hadn't gotten any review. So I instructed them not to present that report and their conclusions to the principals.

It was a meeting that I prepared the agenda for. They are supposed to support me in information and tracking data, which they did. They did their normal briefing, presented their normal information, but I did not want the conclusions of that report briefed to those principals because it was—as far as I was concerned, it hadn't been verified, and it was inconclusive. I don't brief my staff and principals at meetings on things that we haven't verified that are factual yet.

Mr. ZELIFF. If this report was so badly put together and so misinforming and, according to you and also General McCaffrey, that it was not good data, good research——

Admiral KRAMEK. I wouldn't say it was bad data, bad research, or poorly put together. I would say it had not been completed, it was draft No. 2. I think they appeared before you today with draft No. 4, which is still a draft. It hadn't been accepted. It hadn't been completely reviewed.

Mr. ZELIFF. Do you agree with the basic conclusions then relative to the RAND study and also with basic conclusions on interdiction?

Admiral KRAMEK. I don't agree with any one report, whether it be the RAND study or the IDA report, that supports one notion that there is a major silver bullet that will help our drug problem is a valid report.

I think we have to take into account all of the information available and have a balanced approach on treatment, prevention, interdiction, source country programs. They all have to be worked concurrently, and it takes a tremendous bipartisan effort to make that happen, and that will be the only thing that will give the American people the will to win, and we will be able to make some progress.

Mr. ZELIFF. On the RAND data specifically, because that was contained in the report, do you agree or not agree with criticism of the RAND data?

Admiral KRAMEK. My comments to IDA are that I neither agreed nor disagreed. Rather, I thought it was inappropriate for them and I, as Interdiction Coordinator, to report on a RAND report which was a demand side report, and it appeared to me they were trying to enhance their own report. Rather, I directed them to concentrate on interdiction data and report on that, and if that was valid and withstood peer review, whatever they put forth would stand on its own two feet.

I thought it was inappropriate in a report to me to comment on demand data. I am a supply side manager on this war on drugs. I am the Interdiction Coordinator, and, to me, the information they were trying to present on RAND data didn't belong in an interdiction report to me.

Mr. ZELIFF. Captain Boyer, I guess, independently of you, wrote and said, good work on this report.

Admiral KRAMEK. He recommended they take that information out. This is good work, and I would agree, I think they have done a lot of work. They have taken a lot of data, 30,000 data points. They figured out how to smooth it and present it. They must have done a good job.

We have been holding hearings on this. Certainly this—we have given this report more attention than any other report recently that has been put out by any other analyst. It is certainly controversial.

Mr. ZELIFF. My personal conclusion to this, before I turn it over to Mr. Mica, I think we probably—I mean, Mr. Cummings.

Mr. CUMMINGS. I am still here.

Mr. ZELIFF. We will live through this. I guess my conclusion would be, maybe we are doing too many reports and too many studies, and we need people like yourself who basically know what we need to do to win the war on drugs, who, frankly, in terms of interdiction, you previously testified before this subcommittee you have been pretty much right on.

I guess where we go from here, if in the final analysis we start putting more money into interdiction and source country programs and stop cutting them to the bone, and we take a realistic review of whether treatment is really working or whether it isn't, if we return some of those assets we took away in 1992 and 1993 when we really were doing some good things, then I guess it doesn't matter whether people heard the wrong thing outside the room or whatever. I think the important thing is, we move on and start winning the war on drugs. That is what I really care about. And you have done some really great things.

I just wish that somehow, you know, we had a little bit of discussions, some more information as they were putting the appropriations bills together. We probably would have given you more assets. I think we feel a little bit more confident that we would get a better bang for the buck.

With that, I will turn it over to my good friend, Mr. Cummings.

Mr. CUMMINGS. Thank you very much.

I, too, share the feelings of our chairman with regard to your integrity, and your efforts. One of the most moving days of my life was one of my first hearings here, was when you and some of your subordinates came in and talked about your efforts and what you had to do in the waters and various oceans and whatever.

And I went back to my community, and they were very skeptical about what was being done. When I told them about some of the stories you told and your efforts and putting your lives on the line, they were very moved. I want you to continue doing what you are doing.

Let me ask you just a few questions because—and I want to comment on another thing. The word "liar" is a very, very serious word, in my estimation. As a criminal lawyer for 20 years, a trial lawyer, that is not some word that I use lightly. I want you to understand my questions.

I have not heard anybody lie today. I mean—and I have a listening ear for inconsistencies. I think basically what we had was some people that even admitted there was some conjecture, that they had opinions, things they didn't even hear. They heard loud voices in a room, that kind of thing. That is not enough to accuse anybody publicly on C–SPAN of lying. I have a major problem with that because people's reputations are most important.

Having said that, let me ask you this: Did General McCaffrey at any time, to your knowledge, ever try to thwart this effort to get this report out? Did you get that impression, or do you know that?

Admiral KRAMEK. No; he did not. He did not agree with the fundamental premise of the report, but he knew that it hadn't gotten peer review, and he ordered that peer review be obtained for it, which was done, and it was done, and all the results of that—most of the results of that have been submitted to this committee.

Mr. CUMMINGS. One of the things that you said that caught me off guard, and I have to ask you about this, you talk about this TIC——

Admiral KRAMEK. It is a committee headed up by the Commissioner of Customs and for years had been co-chaired by the commandant of the Coast Guard. It has two functions. First, it reports border interdiction philosophy and strategy to the drug czar. It reports directly to ONDCP. And its second function is, it acts as coordinator of the different issues that come up in interdiction that I can't coordinate and solve by myself. These are the bosses, if you will, of almost all of the agencies who are involved in interdiction.

Mr. CUMMINGS. Would you say these people more or less have become experts over time with regard to interdiction?

Admiral KRAMEK. It is the Commissioner of the Customs and Administrator of the DEA.

Mr. CUMMINGS. They have a great interest in interdiction; is that correct?

Admiral KRAMEK. That is their job, and they advise me, and I brought this report to them 2 months before I brought it to the drug czar.

Mr. CUMMINGS. You are going a little fast for me. You presented this report before it even got to the czar; is that right?

Admiral KRAMEK. Over 2 months before it got to him.

Mr. CUMMINGS. And they had the same opinion, it needed some peer review?

Admiral KRAMEK. Stronger than that. They said the report was incomplete, there weren't enough data points; it needed a lot of work. They invited the analyst to get together with their agencies. They needed more data from Health and Human Services, and I tried to get that for him. It needed a lot of work.

Mr. CUMMINGS. By the time you got to the drug czar, you had already had some opinions from TIC?

Admiral KRAMEK. Opinions from the top interdiction coordinator administrators——

Mr. CUMMINGS. I am curious, did you already talk to TIC and this is what they said, or did you go and present your information?

Admiral KRAMEK. TIC's opinion was—but this was something he had to know was a work in progress, because it presented data that hadn't been compared before. In particular, it was focusing on Green Clover, which was an operation that General McCaffrey read at SOUTHCOM.

Mr. CUMMINGS. You told the drug czar that?

Admiral KRAMEK. Oh, yes, I showed him that exactly.

Mr. CUMMINGS. Would it have surprised you if the drug czar's decision had differed from TIC? In other words, if you said all of this to the drug czar and the drug czar said, "I don't care about what TIC says, let's get this out immediately," would that have surprised you?

Admiral KRAMEK. I think what would have surprised me is if he had totally gone against what the interdiction committee was recommending, which was peer review, that the report wasn't ready to be published and that the data hadn't been sufficiently developed.

Mr. CUMMINGS. There has been a lot made of this whole line of debate. Did the drug czar ever say to you, "I don't ever want this to see the light of day?"

Admiral KRAMEK. No, that was never said.

Mr. CUMMINGS. I don't have anything else.

Mr. ZELIFF. Thank you, Mr. Cummings.

Mr. Mica.

Mr. MICA. Thank you, Mr. Chairman.

Did General McCaffrey say to you, "Not a word of this report is to get out"?

Admiral KRAMEK. I can't hear you, sir.

Mr. MICA. Did General McCaffrey say that not a word of this was to get out?

Admiral KRAMEK. No, he never said that.

Mr. MICA. In the March meeting?

Admiral KRAMEK. No; it was May, May 7, May 8. That is when we met.

Mr. MICA. Was there a meeting in March?

Admiral KRAMEK. No. There was only a meeting in May, and I presented the draft findings of the report, that IDA was waiting in his office to give him a full briefing on May 8.

Mr. MICA. You did not meet with General McCaffrey?

Mr. KRAMEK. I did not present the IDA report to him in March, not that I recall. I believe it was May 8.

Mr. MICA. The document we have says the draft final, May 1996. Is this the report? Are you sure about that now?

Now, when you were driving—you were driving back, did you make a comment or did one of your assistants make a comment that not a word of this report is to get out after meeting with the general?

Admiral KRAMEK. I never made that comment. I did not drive back with them, so I wouldn't know if anyone made that comment or who it was.

Mr. MICA. But it wasn't you, and you didn't hear that remark made in the room when you spent time with the general?

Admiral KRAMEK. No. In fact, what I specifically told IDA was that they were not to present the conclusions of the report the next day to the principals' group at the Pentagon, the meeting that I had called of all of these commanders, because the data was still inconclusive and had to have peer review, so I told him not to present it.

Mr. MICA. You had called that meeting, and they were prepared to have that meeting that next day, right, and hear that report?

Admiral KRAMEK. That is correct.

Mr. MICA. Before that, you had decided to have that meeting, present that report, what influenced you not to—to change your mind and suddenly not have that meeting?

Admiral KRAMEK. Two things influenced me. The first thing that influenced me was that the interdiction committee still had not changed their mind, felt the report had not been vetted. And I presented the preliminary, my version of it, to General McCaffrey. He disagreed with it and asked me——

Mr. MICA. He influenced that decision then, somewhat. If you hadn't met with him, you would have been presenting that report; right?

Admiral KRAMEK. I am not sure that I would have.

Mr. MICA. The meeting would have gone on without you?

Admiral KRAMEK. What meeting is that?

Mr. MICA. The meeting you said you canceled the next day.

Admiral KRAMEK. The meeting was the second day of a 2-day conference. Of the 8 hours of that meeting, it was a one-half-hour presentation of an 8-hour meeting.

Mr. MICA. This report wasn't vetted. Did you also testify you first presented this report in January 1996?

Admiral KRAMEK. To the TIC, that is correct, draft 1.

Mr. MICA. But it hadn't been vetted, and you don't remember a meeting in March, right, after he took over as drug czar, McCaffrey took over as drug czar and presented——

Admiral KRAMEK. I think it was in May when I first presented it to him.

Mr. MICA. You don't remember anyone making those comments. Were you aware of any efforts by the drug czar's office to keep this report from coming to Congress?

Admiral KRAMEK. None.

Mr. MICA. Did you see any memos that said this should not be in any way, any of this information, unleashed to Congress?

Admiral KRAMEK. No. I don't recall.

Mr. MICA. Did you produce any memos that said that this report should not be released in any fashion?

Admiral KRAMEK. The only thing I can recall is that the report had not been completed, it was still a draft; and before we accepted its conclusions, we needed it to be a final report approved from the contractor, by the sponsor, who was DOD.

Mr. MICA. Haven't you been concerned for some time that the cutting of the drug interdiction program was a policy of failure, and didn't you see results in your responsibility, your areas of responsibility in the Coast Guard, in and around Puerto Rico, for example, dramatic drug increases and——

Admiral KRAMEK. Yes, I did.

Mr. MICA. Did you take action? Didn't you write Lee Brown, the drug czar in 1994, and express your alarm and also ask for a meeting with the President and the National Security Advisor because you thought it was getting so serious that in fact—let me read—"priority of counternarcotrafficking is a threat to the national security of the United States?"

Did you express that concern to the drug—the former drug czar?

Admiral KRAMEK. I absolutely did, but I would like to explain in what context it was expressed, because I think it was a very important Presidential decision.

Directive 14, that I explained to you, which gave the four primary objectives to achieve, also spoke to a gradual change in strategy. It was called a gradual shift from interdiction in the transit zone to source country.

The IDA report focuses on the effect of source country interdiction—if you will, things like disrupting the air bridge and its potential effect, in their view, on price, purity, and demand.

What had not taken place was the shift. The President's strategy had not been implemented either by the agencies or by the Congress. Rather, interdiction resources had been reduced, as shown on curves previously at this hearing, and resources not put into source country programs. In fact, source country programs had been reduced at the same time.

So the memo I wrote to Dr. Brown, which you cite, was that we should not continue to reduce interdiction resources; rather, we should bring them back up to prior years' levels until the source country's strategy was effective and investments were made in the source countries, which I believe is an effective strategy.

So what had happened was, a gradual shift didn't take place. We cut interdiction, didn't make the investment in the source strategy, and I saw that as problematic and advised the drug czar of that.

Mr. MICA. You knew we were headed for disaster, then?

Admiral KRAMEK. I wouldn't say "disaster," but it was in the wrong direction.

Mr. MICA. Let me ask you, too, about the cocaine. It declined from a peak of 70,000 kilograms in 1992 to 37,000 kilograms in 1995; is that correct?

Admiral KRAMEK. That is correct.

Mr. MICA. What is the Coast Guard's responsibility in regard to Puerto Rico? Isn't it to guard the waters around Puerto Rico?

Admiral KRAMEK. Our responsibility in Puerto Rico is the same as it is everywhere in the maritime area; the Coast Guard is the lead agency for interdicting drugs in the maritime area.

Mr. MICA. Hadn't your resources been dramatically cut by Congress? And I have the amounts of——

Admiral KRAMEK. By approximately 40 to 50 percent over the last 4 years.

Mr. MICA. Forty to fifty percent, and this was from 1993 to 1995.

Admiral KRAMEK. Basically, from probably 1991 or 1992 to 1995; that is correct.

Mr. MICA. I have 1992 to 1995, when the other party controlled the Congress and made those decisions, and what you announced this morning was the resumption of your program in Puerto Rico. And isn't it true that this subcommittee—the chairman took our subcommittee to Puerto Rico to examine this problem?

Admiral KRAMEK. You held a hearing based on a GAO study that indicated 28 percent of narcotics, particularly cocaine, came through the Puerto Rico area of responsibility. This spring, I testified at that hearing. Subsequently, the chairman held a field hearing in Puerto Rico.

Mr. MICA. Wasn't the conclusion that there was a serious problem there?

Mr. KRAMEK. I was very happy that the committee paid attention to the GAO study and held the field hearing; I thought it was excellent. But I would point out that I had made Puerto Rico a major issue to the drug czar almost a year ago——

Mr. MICA. And nothing was done.

Admiral KRAMEK. I had pointed that out to General McCaffrey the first time I met with him, and the supplemental appropriation that the President sent to Congress in April requested funds for the Coast Guard to do the Puerto Rican operations. I believe that was about the same time you were holding the hearings, if not before.

I think we are all on the same wavelength, but what you have done has certainly helped.

Mr. MICA. General McCaffrey said he was afraid the report would be throwing him a bouquet. I was concerned that the report would be throwing him a bomb.

Admiral KRAMEK. The GAO report, that is?

Mr. MICA. No; the IDA report. It reported more concentration on interdiction and source depression of the drug trade.

Admiral KRAMEK. There is no question, and I have testified before this committee before, that we were short of resources to do interdiction in the transit zone, short of resources to do interdiction and finance source country programs. I think, in over 10 hearings, you have created a public record, and I applaud this particular committee and its oversight in doing that, for showing that we need to do more to accomplish goals No. 4 and 5 of the strategy.

I will say that I recently, the first week in August, got all of the commanders together again in the Pentagon for 2 days. I had them review the new 1996 strategy General McCaffrey has presented to this committee. I asked them what they—their major issues were in not being able to implement that strategy. Approximately one-third of those issues were resource-related issues, all of which were requested in the President's supplemental request in April, and I believe now, all of which you financed at the conclusion of this last week's omnibus appropriations bill.

Mr. MICA. I will repeat one more time: You did not hear General McCaffrey say that not a word of this report was to get out?

Admiral KRAMEK. No, he never said that, to my knowledge.

Mr. MICA. Mr. Chairman, it may be necessary to refer a matter of conflict that we have heard before our investigations—direct conflict in testimony, to the Justice Department. And I would like to consult with staff and with you on this matter. And I think that it should be further explored and it should be further considered by our subcommittee.

Mr. ZELIFF. I will take that under advisement.

Your time has expired.

Admiral, I showed this to General McCaffrey, but let me just point out—and you are familiar with these numbers, I am sure: Interdiction efforts, we showed $2 billion in 1991; $1.9 million in 1992; $1.5 million in 1993; $1.3 million in 1994; $1.2 million in 1995; $1.13 million in 1996.

I also referred to a U.S. interdiction coordinator memorandum of 1995 that you wrote in June, listing all the assets that were pulled out of the drug war.

And I only have one motivation here and the motivation is, where are we going? You know, we have discussed that on several occasions, what has happened since 1992 in terms of interdiction—where we have had a success, where we are going, what we need.

We have made some changes. You are fairly familiar with the resources we put in the current budget for 1997. How do you feel about that?

Admiral KRAMEK. I think we are going in the right direction.

Mr. ZELIFF. Is there a stop sign 100 yards out? Have we done enough, or are we winning this thing?

I have been at a couple of Coast Guard functions as well as a lot of functions around, and I ask people, are we winning the drug war? and I don't see any hands go up.

Tell me from your heart, where are we going and what is it going to take and are we doing enough?

Admiral KRAMEK. If you would call it a war, we are winning the war on drugs. I have to look at——

Mr. ZELIFF. Why wouldn't we call it a war?

Admiral KRAMEK. Some people don't like to call it a war. I will call it a war, because I think it is.

We need a couple of elements to win. I think we are winning, when you take a look over the last 10 years, when I take a look at the amount, overall, in the population that drug use has gone down and what has happened in the United States. I still think it is a major problem, No. 1 or 2 on the list with the American people.

I think most of our major crime is—at least 60 percent of it is directly related to drug abuse. I think that General McCaffrey—in fact, I know—is putting us back on track with a balanced approach that we have to do all of these things concurrently—treatment, prevention, core-country programs, interdiction.

I feel we are short in interdiction. It is only 9 or 10 percent of the total budget; I have testified before it needs to be probably around 13 or 14 percent. I think the President's supplemental reflects that and your record shows that, and I think we are headed in the right direction.

The action Congress took on an appropriations bill this year is in the right direction, and I am hopeful that when the agencies analyze what took place in Congress and as they are preparing their 1998 budgets, that they will ask for the remainder that is necessary to have a robust interdiction and source-country program to complement our treatment and prevention and education program.

Mr. ZELIFF. How much more is necessary?

Admiral KRAMEK. As of April of this year, probably $250 to $350 million was necessary. The President's supplemental requested $250 million. I am not sure how much Congress appropriated this weekend, because my staff is still sorting that out because it came in many different accounts. But I think we are getting very close, Mr. Chairman.

Mr. ZELIFF. And you feel that with that number, that brings us up to 13 or 14 percent?

Admiral KRAMEK. I think it should bring us close to 13 percent as a portion of the total pie. I have not had a chance to analyze that.

Should we go back to the $3 billion or whatever the top chart was in 1992? No. At that particular time, those numbers are a little bit skewed. We were buying equipment; we were buying sensors; we were buying intelligence systems. We don't have OPTEMPO, ship time, plane time. The Coast Guard has been reduced by 4,000 people and $400 million a year over the last 3 years in order to meet our balanced budget requirements.

Mr. ZELIFF. I think, though, with all due respect, sir, that we do have to balance our budget, but we are putting assets and putting priorities on the drug war in spite of that.

Admiral KRAMEK. We are certainly trying to do both, as you know, Mr. Chairman. I think both can be done. We made some major adjustments.

You asked me what it would take. It will take those assets, those resources; but more than that, it will take a bipartisan effort to keep this in front of the American people, because it is going to take all of us together on educating our children, making it a national priority, providing the resources to the agencies, whether it is education, prevention, interdiction, or source country, and one heck of a lot of cooperation by our foreign partners.

You cannot accomplish source-country programs without total cooperation with Peru, Bolivia, Colombia, and Venezuela. You were there; I was there.

One thing you haven't talked about that is most important when you talk about all of this IDA data, the reason we disrupted the air bridge wasn't IDA data. IDA certainly gave us all the air tracks in that particular area.

It was clear that by disrupting that bridge it would drive the price of coca paste—60 percent of all the coca leaves in the world are grown in Peru; 80 percent of all the cocaine that comes to the United States comes from those coca leaves that gets transported to Colombia for processing. If we could disrupt that, it would drive the price of coca leaves below normal crops like pineapples, bananas, and soybeans.

And that's exactly what President Fujimori needed to develop an alternative crop program. That transpired, as you know—you probably met with him, too, and he probably told you the same thing.

We achieved that with Operation Laser Strike at this particular time.

Mr. ZELIFF. Wasn't there—weren't we feuding with President Fujimori over a period of maybe 2 years and didn't we finally agree to support that policy and weren't there some problems prior to the air bridge?

Admiral KRAMEK. Well, there were problems prior to the air bridge because he was at war with Ecuador, No. 1, and some of the equipment that he would need to prosecute his end on the war on drugs, there was some thoughts that he might have to be—using it for military needs, and all of those other State Department-related policies which come into play.

I think we have a pretty clear path on what Peru is doing now in cooperation with the United States to shut the air bridge down.

Mr. ZELIFF. Mr. Mica.

Mr. MICA. Mr. Chairman, just a couple of closing comments. First, I want to thank you for holding this hearing. I think it's important that we look at this whole question of success of interdiction, of trying to attack the narcotics problem and trafficking and source countries and transit zones and other questions that have been raised here.

I am still very concerned and very alarmed that, in fact, that this subcommittee that deals with oversight on this issue that has been working so closely with these agencies, did not get a copy of this report. I am even more concerned that this report was still—was originally vetted in January.

I am very concerned that the report has been massaged to death, that—and it was kept from us during a critical period when we were making decisions on the direction of policy, again in a time of limited resources, with our taxpayers footing the bill, and with seeing the results of a disastrous policy on our streets and with our children.

So I thank you for holding the hearing. I regret that I don't think we have gotten the whole story, the rest of the story, as Paul Harvey says, and I think we need to look at this and we also need to keep these folks on track.

But I thank you, as our last hearing probably together at least in Washington, for your tremendous leadership, what you have done, your personal sacrifices and your commitment to do this at tremendous personal cost to yourself and your family. But you have—you are responsible for getting this moving, and I am dismayed again, by what I have seen here today.

Thank you so much.

Mr. ZELIFF. Thank you.

And I think it has been very much of a group effort with a whole bunch of people getting it back on track.

I guess my last question, admiral, is how do you judge success? How do you figure out whether we are on the right track, in terms of interdiction? Do you have quantifiable goals? And maybe just kind of—you know, do you have a lot of assets at your disposal?

Admiral KRAMEK. The total measure of success, to me, is only one measurement that needs to take place, and to look at our overall population and as a combination of all the programs that we have mentioned, including interdiction, the measure of success would be if drug use in the United States declines.

If drug use in the United States doesn't decline through all of the populations, not just our children, but the casual users and different elements of our population, then the entire program is not successful.

Mr. ZELIFF. I thank you very much.

I appreciate your testimony today and again to your commitment to your country and not only in the drug war but in your total commitment. Again, my comments to you earlier still stand. I have tremendous respect for you and the uniform you wear, and I think you are one of our great assets, and I wish you well.

Admiral KRAMEK. Thank you, Mr. Chairman.

Mr. ZELIFF. We are going to combine the last two panels, if we can. I will just introduce as those folks come forward. I would like to welcome Dr. Tom Snitch.

Dr. Snitch is currently president of Little Falls Associates, Inc., and director of Federal research programs for Golden Gate University. Formerly he was a senior methodology expert at the National Academy of Sciences.

Dr. Snitch, we thank you for being here today.

At this point, I would also like to welcome Dr. Peter Reuter—Reuter.

Mr. REUTER. Reuter.

Mr. ZELIFF. Dr. Reuter is a professor at the University of Maryland School of Public Affairs. Formerly he served as co-director of the Drug Policy Research Center at the RAND Corp.

Dr. Reuter, thank you for being here today.

Mr. REUTER. Thank you.

Mr. ZELIFF. Why don't we start with you, Dr. Snitch.

If you would stand, I need to swear you in, if you would.

[Witnesses sworn.]

Mr. ZELIFF. If you would like to condense your testimony, if you would, and the balance of your written testimony will certainly be accepted for the record.

STATEMENTS OF THOMAS H. SNITCH, PH.D., PRESIDENT, LITTLE FALLS ASSOCIATES, INC.; AND PETER REUTER, PH.D., PROFESSOR, UNIVERSITY OF MARYLAND

Mr. SNITCH. Thank you, Mr. Chairman.

I only want to make a few quick points here.

It has been, No. 1, a rather long day and, No. 2——

Mr. ZELIFF. It has been an interesting day, though; hasn't it?

Mr. SNITCH. Very interesting. And even more important, in my terms, I am very anxious to find out what the Baltimore Orioles are doing since they started 2 hours ago and the game should just about be over by now. So I would like to see what the Orioles did today.

Your task to me was to examine the methodological soundness and basically cite to the veracity of the IDA study. I took a look at this study, the RAND study, and some of the critiques that were provided to me. And I look at this, at this assignment, and I take the position of being a social scientist.

My background and training is in methodological approaches and how to develop rigorous analytical ways to study empirical data sets and then to apply those approaches to looking at significant international policy issues.

I am not, by any means, a drug expert. I instead take a look at this as from a methodological point of view, and I try to look at some of the ways that if you came to me and asked me some of the questions that were presented today and asked of IDA, how would I go about providing you with those answers in a rigorous scientific fashion.

I just want to make three quick points and then we can open it up for some questions.

After reading the IDA study, I think that given the assumptions that were placed on the study, the data issues, and we can talk about that more later, which I think is one of the real key issues here, if you look at how they approached this issue and when you really come down to it, what IDA is trying to do is to provide empirical data to what I would argue is almost a common sense or intuitive argument. That is, if you were to say to me, if you were to decrease the supply of drugs coming into the United States from Latin America, would you expect that that would in some way have a resultant impact on the amount of supply of drugs available and, therefore, if the amount of supply of drugs is changed, would that affect the price?

If you were to ask me that question, I would say that sounds logical to me. But if you look at from it a scientific point of view, I would have to go back and collect empirical data and try to verify the correctness of that supposition.

I think the IDA is basically doing some cutting-edge research, because they are looking at some very difficult variables and some very difficult data collection issues which I think are important to provide into this whole debate over drug strategy.

If you look and just try and imagine, if you were to ask me what is the street price of cocaine in the United States, how would you go about finding out what that was, well, we have all sorts of data points here. They are from DEA data that was collected from people who were out there making supposed buys for this.

I suppose we could go out and ask people in prisons how much they charged or how much they paid for cocaine, or perhaps we could even go out on the street and try to create a data collection survey, something that I don't think I would want to do, that is, ask buyers and sellers of cocaine how much they were charging.

But what they have done here is tried to look at a longitudinal study, that is, the price of cocaine on the street over time, and look at fluctuations. And if you look at their graphs, you will see that indeed there are marked changes in the price of cocaine on the streets of the United States.

The question then comes down to: What causes those changes? I think what IDA is trying to look at—and I don't think that in their conclusions they would state that interdiction is the only reason that you find prices increasing on the streets, but that interdiction efforts have had some type of impact on the price of cocaine in the United States.

Now, we can argue all you want about price elasticities of demand and we can look at what is the elasticity of a heavy user vis-a-vis a light user? But I think what IDA is trying to do is set the stage in terms of putting an issue on the table for discussion to look and try to quantify the impact of source interdiction as it applies to actual pricing mechanisms.

So I think that there are some flaws and some analysis that they have done in their study that I might do a little differently, but overall I think it's a very useful effort. I think, as a scientist, I would like to see studies like this put on the table for open discussion, and I think much of the discussion here in the hearings today has been very useful.

From a more editorial point of view, I would just say that from what I understand, this is a federally funded study. It is unclassified, and I think that it behooves both myself as a scientist and myself as a taxpayer to have the ability to look at these studies when we begin to debate policy issues. And, therefore, I see no reason why this study shouldn't be released and shouldn't be available for public discussion among interested parties.

Thank you.

Mr. ZELIFF. Thank you.

Mr. Reuter.

Mr. REUTER. Thank you very much, Mr. Chairman.

I ask my written statement be placed in the record.

Mr. ZELIFF. Without objection.

Mr. REUTER. As you stated, I was at RAND for some years and was involved in the management of the study that is referred to here as the RAND study. I probably provided some of the intellectual underpinnings for it in the earlier study I did of interdiction for the Department of Defense in 1988.

The IDA study is, in fact, very simple. It begins by asserting that there was a marked success in drug policy in 1989. The IDA researchers observed that the price of cocaine, which had fallen sharply throughout the 1980's, stabilized after 1989. That was defined as a success because the researchers claimed that absent some newly effective Government intervention, the price of cocaine would have fallen to $25, less than half the figure they estimated it stabilized at in 1989.

This is absolutely critical to the whole analysis. This is no longer facts. This is a theoretical projection on their part. The only basis they offer for that projection is a statement by Mark Moore, a professor at Harvard, about what the price of cocaine would be if legal, and a statement that: "Exponential decay in prices might be expected for a commodity in a saturated market characterized by unconstrained competition."

I have no idea where that statement comes from and no references provided for it. It may, indeed, be that looking at the drift of prices as a physicist, you would indeed see that decline, but in economics there's no basis for making that statement.

The next question that the IDA researchers asked was: What would explain this apparent success? I will for the moment leave aside their claim that there was a success.

Their answer was that this success must be the result of more effective interdiction efforts by the United States and producer countries, since they claimed there were three upturns in the price series they had constructed that occurred shortly after the launch of three interdiction operations. From this they concluded that interdiction operations should be credited with all reductions in cocaine consumption resulting from the price increase that they inferred; did not measure, they inferred.

Interdiction then seemed to be an extraordinarily cost-effective program achieving a 1 percent reduction in cocaine consumption for only $8 million. This contrasts dramatically with a RAND estimate that source country and interdiction programs require $350 to $800 million to accomplish that same reduction. There is no basis for this.

Their measurement of price—sorry. There is no basis for this because, in fact, there were many other things that effect the price of cocaine. It is not simply driven by Government expenditures on interdiction.

For example, over the last 10 years, an increasing number of persons have been locked up for drug-selling offenses. Presumably, that has some effect on the supply curve for drugs. It has made this business more risky, and one presumes that that has an effect just as interdiction will have an effect by increasing riskiness.

The other central problem of the study is that the measures of price are highly questionable. There are already in existence some well-documented price series published by the Abt Corp. under contract to ONDCP, published over a number of years, well-documented, well-analyzed using exactly the same data.

There's no reference to these series in the IDA study and they show a very different level of prices. That is, the street price of cocaine per pure gram is more like $125 rather than $50 and, just as importantly, they don't show the two upturns in retail cocaine prices that the IDA series shows in 1992 and 1995. There is a modest upturn in 1995, but it is so small that it could simply be noisy—noisy data. These data are not collected by scientists in white coats in sterile labs, or even by clerks writing down numbers from supermarket labels; they come from undercover purchases in markets characterized by lots of cheating and uncertainty.

The IDA study then has a spurious price increase which is in conflict with what is available from other sources.

The other sort of major failing here is that in looking at prices, they look only at what they claim are retail prices. In fact, if interdiction is effective on prices, what you would expect to see is a rise in import prices and then wholesale prices and eventually retail prices. What is made immediately risky and expensive by interdiction is smuggling and smugglers sell not in the retail market but in the wholesale market.

In fact, the Abt series for wholesale shows no such increase in wholesale prices in 1992 or 1995. They continued to decline, and an increase in retail prices is more reasonably attributed to changes in enforcement at the local level or at least domestically, if DEA also operates at that lower level of the market.

My written testimony has a few more details about some of the technical failings of the study, which I think is very weak. The failure of the authors to cite most of the published research on drug prices and markets is simply remarkable.

The claim that these are data that have not been analyzed before is simply untrue. Every price series here, except one, has been regularly published and even that last series, SmithKline Beecham—SmithKline testing data have also been analyzed by at least one other person.

One would at least have expected them to address why their price series looked so different from the price series that had already been published.

Let me conclude by saying that the weakness of this study has no policy meaning whatsoever. Interdiction might indeed be more effective than RAND researchers, including myself, have previously estimated. The volume of research in this area is scandalously small and it's easy to raise questions about the few studies that have been done. I mean, I would say that the RAND study in controlling cocaine is far and away the best study of these issues. That's easy enough. There are no other studies of this issue until this one is actually published.

John Caulkins, a major contributor to work in this area, has undertaken a number of conceptual pieces that I think provide the basis for the next generation of studies in this area that might enrich the results of the RAND work. There is new evidence about the elasticity of prices that suggests that demand is more responsive to price increases than was assumed by the RAND model and by the IDA analysts.

If Congress and high-level decisionmakers in the executive branch make decisions about the allocation of resources amongst Federal drug control programs in a reasonable way, then they will have to push agencies into investing in systematic analysis and data collection.

Thank you.

[The prepared statement of Mr. Reuter follows:]

Testimony of Peter Reuter before the Subcommittee on International Affairs, House Committee on Government Reform October 1, 1996

My name is Peter Reuter. I am a professor in the School of Public Affairs and in the Department of Criminology at the University of Maryland. From 1989 to 1993, I was Co-Director of RAND's Drug Policy Research Center, where I led studies on various aspects of drug policy. In 1988 I was the principal author of a major DoD funded study of the effectiveness of the interdiction program[1]. I appreciate the opportunity to appear before the Committee and to discuss the Institute of Defense Analysis Report entitled *An Empirical Examination of Counterdrug Interdiction Program Effectiveness*.

Given the events that have led to the hearing, I should start by describing my association with both RAND's study entitled *Controlling Cocaine: Demand vs. Supply Programs* (hereafter *Controlling Cocaine)* and the Office of National Drug Control Policy (ONDCP). While I was not an author of the RAND study, I was very much involved in its genesisand provided numerous comments to the researchers. *Controlling Cocaine* also draws on my earlier interdiction study and another paper that I co-authored.[2] I have never been an official consultant to ONDCP but have reviewed the IDA study and at least one other study at their request *pro bono*; I am in discussion with ONDCP at the moment about doing some consulting on measures of effectiveness.

It is important to carry out studies of the effectiveness, and cost effectiveness of various federal drug control programs. The existing studies are very few in number and represent fairly small scale efforts. While I believe that both *Sealing the Borders* and *Controlling Cocaine* are professionally done and credible studies, they are certainly not definitive. Indeed, I shall in the course of my testimony suggest some basic issues that these studies have not explored and which might make a substantial difference to their results.

However the IDA study is not a useful contribution. It is deeply flawed conceptually. Its basic assumption is that only interdiction works and that no other drug control program has affected the price of cocaine; unsurprisingly, interdiction is thus shown to be effective. The empirical work is poorly done, showing a striking lack of familiarity with prior research. The results it produces have no credibility.

---

[1] Reuter, Crawford and Cave *Sealing the Borders* RAND, 1988

[2] Reuter and Kleiman "Risks and Prices" in Morris and Tonry (eds.) *Crime and Justice: A Review of Research* Vol 7, 1986

The IDA Analysis

Summary

Let me begin by summarizing the major problems of the study. The principal conceptual weakness lies in the claim that the retail price of cocaine would, in the absence of effective interdiction programs, have fallen to $25 per pure gram. This is based on a mysterious assertion about the characteristics of drug markets that has no analytic or empirical basis. It also ignores all the other factors, particularly other federal and state enforcement programs, that influence the price of cocaine and leads to a dramatic overstatement of the cost-effectiveness of interdiction.

Empirically, the study is flawed by a failure to interpret a number of data series correctly. The price series confounds domestic wholesale and retail prices, which leads to errors in the behavior of prices over time and may exaggerate the estimated impact of individual interdiction efforts. It makes claims that prices have recently increased for which no data are offered and which are flatly contradicted by others who follow this data series. The misinterpretation of the DAWN (Drug Abuse Warning Network) and DUF (Drug Use Forecasting) series as measures of consumption leads to baffling analyses.

The study shows strikingly little familiarity with the relevant analytic literature, which is readily accessible and of modest volume. It references neither the other models of interdiction nor the growing literature on the behavior and determinants of cocaine prices. This may explain the unsophisticated character of the empirical analyses.

Conceptual Issues.

The study's central assertion is that the retail price of cocaine would, absent effective interdiction, have fallen to about $25 per pure gram. Nothing else contributed to keeping prices from falling to this level. The cost effectiveness equation presented on p.8 implicitly sets the price impact of all other enforcement efforts at zero. I.e. if the federal government were to eliminate all domestic enforcement expenditures, the price of cocaine would not be affected.

The assertion about the potential price of cocaine is justified in two ways.

(1) Citation to an assertion by Mark Moore, a leading analyst of drug policy, that the floor price of cocaine would be $15-20 (p.6). As represented in both the Rydell and Everingham study (which IDA uses as the source of the statement) and the original Moore article[7] this was not a statement about what would happen if interdiction went to zero but about the consequences of

[7]Moore "Supply Reduction. And Drug Law Enforcement" in Wilson and Tonry (eds.) *Drugs and Crime*

legalizing cocaine. Moore is very explicit that factors other than enforcement would contribute to raising the price of cocaine above that legal floor.

(2) A projection from the curvilinear behavior of retail prices in the period 1985 to 1989. No justification is offered for making this projection except that "an exponential decay ..might be expected for a commodity in a saturated market characterized by unconstrained competition." No literature is cited for this latter assertion, which is completely novel to me. I note that one of the other reviewers was similarly baffled as the origin of the claim. There might well be learning by doing that leads to a continuing outward shift in the supply curve as the market expands[8] (i.e. smugglers, like computer manufacturers, become more efficient as they become more experienced) but there is no basis for asserting that this would continue indefinitely. Basically, IDA simply makes an extension of a line on a graph and calls it analysis.

There is thus no basis for the statement that the retail price of cocaine would have fallen to $25 in the absence of interdiction expenditures. Explaining the behavior of cocaine prices over the last 10 years is indeed challenging. It is difficult to understand their continued decline (in inflation adjusted terms, using the Abt series) given the vast increase in the number and length of prison sentences received by cocaine dealers and the apparent stagnation of demand, as shown by the number of frequent users that are not incarcerated. But any effort to explain that pattern would certainly include a modeling of the effect of many programs other than interdiction, such as state and local enforcement, treatment and federal imprisonment which account for very much larger sums than interdiction and (apart from treatment) which clearly impose great risks and cost on drug dealers.

As suggested in my introduction, a more probative method for assessing the impact of specific interdiction programs is to examine the import, rather than retail, price of cocaine. This was the method used in *Sealing the Borders*. Certainly one would expect that the first sign of effective transit zone (and possibly source zone) interdiction would be on the smugglers' margin, as measured by the difference between the import price (at which smugglers sell drugs) and the export price (at which they buy the drugs). IDA makes no reference to this price margin. In fact import prices remain a small share of retail price. In March 1995 DEA reported Chicago kilogram prices (which are higher than the import price, since imports are sold in bundles of 10 to 1,000 kilograms) were $21,000-25,000, while retail prices in that city were $100-150 per gram; adjusting for purity,

---

[8] A model of this kind was developed by J. Cave and P.Reuter in *The Interdictor's Lot* RAND 1988

the retail price was equivalent to $150-200,000 per kilogram[9]. Thus the import price is less than one sixth of the retail price. Moreover the import price seems not to have increased since 1985; indeed, after adjusting for inflation, it has fallen by about one third.

IDA simply fails to model the mechanism by which interdiction affects retail prices. They do not explain whether one should adopt an additive or multiplicative model in projecting from import to retail prices. They manage to do this by simply assuming that the only influence on retail prices is interdiction.

Data Interpretation

The IDA price series shows anomalies compared to those published by other analysts. These anomalies may account for some of the surprising findings on the impact of interdiction.

For example, the series developed by Abt Associates for ONDCP[10] shows substantially higher prices for the post 1989 period. For the period 1991-1993, the upper bound estimate is as high as $168 and the lower bound estimate no lower than $120. In contrast the IDA figures for 1991-1993 in Figure 2, show prices between about $50 and $85 per pure gram. This difference may be explained by the peculiar procedure IDA used to estimate the price series, namely the inclusion of all purchases up to 10 kilograms, which is at least two and possibly three levels above retail level. Given that DEA makes numerous purchases at the higher levels of the market, this series cannot be taken to represent retail prices.

A retailer sells in approximately one gram units and buys in about 10 gram units. A wholesaler buys in 50 to 250 gram units. A high level wholesaler might buy 1 to 10 kilogram units. If, as has been postulated in the risks and prices model, the mark-up at various levels of the market is determined primarily by the intensity of enforcement at that particular level, this price series confounds the effects of different enforcement efforts.

The result is that much of the variation that IDA reports may be an artifact of the mix of observations in the STRIDE data. If in one quarter DEA makes more purchases at the true retail level (i.e. less than 5 grams) the average price for that quarter will go up, even if actual prices have not varied, simply because the price per pure gram is much higher for smaller purchases. This kind of variation is taken account of in other price series developed by Caulkins[11] and Abt.

---

[9] Drug Enforcement Administration *Illegal Drug Price/Purity Report: United States January 1992-March 1995.*
[10] *What America's Users Spend on Illicit Drugs, 1988-1993*
[11] Caulkins *A Price Series for Cocaine* Santa Monica, CA, RAND, 1994

Another odd feature of the price analyses is the failure to take advantage of the regional variation that is available in STRIDE (System to Retrieve Information from Drug Evidence), DAWN and DUF. Prices vary among cities in both absolute levels and fluctuations over time. While it is hard to determine what exactly IDA did in Figure C-1 (Correlation between STRIDE and DUF) there is no suggestion that IDA attempted to generate city level STRIDE data. That leaves two possibilities:

(a) Each city was weighted equally and a DUF average percent positive was estimated for the nation. Thus New York City, with 7 million residents would be weighted equally with Portland, a city with less than half a million.

(b) The cities were analyzed separately but a single national price was used. Unless the time series across cities are highly correlated, which is not my impression, this will generate spurious correlations.

Conclusion

There are numerous major and minor errors in the study which I had not had time to fully describe. For example, the estimates of the elasticity of demand violate the basic rules of econometrics text books; since however IDA ended up using the same elasticity as *Controlling Cocaine*, this is of little relevance, except for the doubt that it casts on the qualifications of the researchers. The choice of 1989 as a starting point for the finding of effective source zone interdiction is justified by a series of non-sequiturs[12].

The IDA study is simply not credible. Every page shows a lack of expertise and analytic competence in the relevant areas. I have never seen a study which so comprehensively betrayed one of the basic rules of scientific research, namely read the literature. *Controlling Cocaine* was replete with the basic references; the IDA team ignored them all. If they had located Caulkins' conjecture about multiplicative effects of import price increases, they would have had a much better basis for beginning a critique of *Controlling Cocaine*; they had read so little that they seem to have been unaware of it.

The weaknesses of this study have no policy significance. It may indeed be the case that too little is spent on interdiction. I suggested that possibility in testimony on May 1, 1996 to the

---

[12] "Prior to 1988, the U.S. Customs Service and other law enforcement agencies aggressively conducted a campaign to stop the aerial transportation of cocaine across the borders of the U.S. While those efforts were highly successful in stopping the aerial influx, there is no evidence of price increases in the U.S.

Senate Judiciary Committee, though I would be surprised if the increase would constitute a large share of the total federal drug budget. To make that assessment the federal government, including the major enforcement agencies, would have to consistently invest in developing data and analysis that would provide Congress and other high level policy makers with the ability to compare the cost-effectiveness of different programs.

No such effort has been made. For example, no agency consistently reports data on leaf prices, or indeed prices of cocaine as it moves from the farm to export, which is essential to any analysis of foreign drug control efforts. IDA's only comment on leaf prices was based on a report from Reuters News Agency (no relative), published in the *Washington Times*; surely the agencies of the United States can provide something more authoritative than for a research contractor. Nor do agencies such as Customs, Coast Guard and DEA develop policy analytic expertise, either internally or with external contractors.

Evidence Based Research (EBR) conducted a study of the cost-effectiveness of interdiction for ONDCP in 1996. The EBR study remains classified; only a summary has been released, which does not permit a full assessment of its validity, though I remain skeptical of any study which does not take into account prices, instead relying on some measure of disruption imposed on smugglers. In 1987 WEFA, a well respected economic consulting firm, did a study of the cost-effectiveness of interdiction for the Customs Service, comparing it to other types of domestic law enforcement[13]. It has disappeared from sight because it was obviously biased toward finding interdiction more effective and used transparently inappropriate measures. Otherwise, apart from classified studies that I might not have seen, there are only *Sealing the Borders*, which made no comparisons with other programs, and *Controlling Cocaine* to guide Congress in its assessment of the effectiveness of interdiction.

The federal government does indeed fund quite a large program of drug policy evaluation research but almost exclusively for treatment and prevention programs. These demand side programs may receive only one third of the federal drug budget but they probably account for ninety percent of the federally funded evaluation. The explanation is no mystery; treatment lacks political friends and is always being subject to scrutiny to show that it "works". No such scrutiny is required of federal enforcement programs.

---

market from these efforts. We thus conclude that the effects of U.S. border interdiction are included and accounted for in the general exponential decline of price prior to 1989." (p.7)

[13] Godshaw, Koppel and Pancoast

This surely provides an utterly inadequate basis for decisions about the allocation of the federal drug budget, now in excess of $15 billion, if agency figures are to be trusted[14] and dominated by big federal enforcement efforts Though acknowledging my self-interest in the matter, I think that one good outcome from the IDA fiasco might be an awareness on the part of both the Executive branch and Congress that more money has to be invested to answer these complex questions about the cost-effectiveness of drug enforcement programs in an objective and defensible manner.

I would be happy to answer any questions.

[14] On this matter see Murphy *Keeping the Score: The Frailties of the Federal Drug Control Budget* RAND, 1994

Mr. ZELIFF. Thank you very much.

Mr. Hastert.

Mr. HASTERT. Thank you, Mr. Chairman.

At least very quickly, I was interested in your presentation, Dr. Reuter. You used words like scurrilous and scandalous.

Mr. REUTER. Say that again?

Mr. HASTERT. Scurrilous is a word that you used.

Mr. REUTER. I don't think I used the word scurrilous.

Mr. HASTERT. You did.

Mr. REUTER. Spurious.

Mr. HASTERT. I thought it was scurrilous.

Mr. REUTER. No, it was spurious.

Mr. HASTERT. Well, all right.

Well, I just wondered if there was empirical evidence to put a qualitative face on what is scurrilous and what is scandalous in your empirical evidence.

Mr. REUTER. I am sorry. I simply was referring to something being a spurious correlation, a spurious observation. It is nothing about—not impugning——

Mr. HASTERT. Anyway, you used the word scandalous, too. That's fine. I thought that was rather unscientific.

Dr. Snitch, in your estimate of the IDA study, were good scientific data used?

Mr. SNITCH. They used the data that was available. As was just stated, the data collections in this area are few and far between, and I think it's rather difficult sometimes to get very good data on what actually is the price of cocaine on the street at any given time. As I said before, if you look at their analysis over time, I believe that they used the best data that was available to them and did their analysis with that. Yes, sir.

Mr. HASTERT. So how about the conclusions that they drew from it? Are they sound conclusions or not?

Mr. SNITCH. I would argue that the conclusions, as I have read this study and looking at the data and the restraints that they were working under—I don't know what IDA's tasking order originally was and what they were asked to look at. But if you follow the study, as they have carried it out, I think that their conclusions can be substantiated by the data, yes, sir.

Mr. HASTERT. Well, my understanding is that they were doing studies—they started out, you know, as a physicist doing this study but they found that they were looking at over-the-surface—over-the-horizon radar and they got involved in tracking drug planes and they found out when they started to put a real tight kibosh on drug trafficking that there was a reaction in the market. So I guess that's how they got started.

I'm not sure if—that probably, as an economist we would want models and everything else to fit in there, but there is an action and reaction, so to speak, which I guess the physicists look at this.

And can you say that after you look at this evidence that there is a cause and an effect here?

Mr. SNITCH. I see correlations on the data that was presented. Trying to determine causality is much more difficult. I think you have to go into a multivaried analysis type of situation. But, again, in looking at the data, when they—when they show you data and pricing over time, and then they superimpose upon that data various external events, that is, interdiction efforts, and you see a short time lag and then you start to see increases in prices. Maybe that may be coincidence, but nonetheless, it is showing that there is a trend evident on their data.

Mr. HASTERT. And we are sitting here trying to make policy, long-term policy. It might be a year, 2 years, maybe 5 years. And, you know, we don't have perfect data to make any decision on. Part of it comes from the——

Mr. SNITCH. Sir, I don't think you will ever get perfect data. That's probably not the issue. It is what is the best data you can have.

As I said in my remarks earlier, I think it would have been very useful for you if you would have had this study and this debate that we are having today perhaps 4 months ago or 5 months ago, before you got into appropriations and authorizations and policy issues, as opposed to the day after the new fiscal year started.

Mr. HASTERT. Well, I agree.

Well, we have another fiscal year coming up. But I was the person who had to try to persuade or discuss it with a lot of Appropriation Subcommittee chairmen.

Thank you.

I want to yield back, Mr. Chairman.

Mr. ZELIFF. I thank you, Mr. Hastert.

Mr. HASTERT. Mr. Chairman, if I could, too, let me just take a second.

Maybe this may be the appropriate time, maybe not, but you know I have been able to work with you and this committee for a lot of years and especially the last year or so have worked on this issue. You have been an exemplary and very fine leader on this issue.

I think a lot of the things that have been done today and happened in this whole issue would not have happened if not your leadership had taken place. So I just want to say from the bottom of my heart, and I know a lot of those people that are out there, that this makes a real difference, too.

Thank you.

I know that you are not going to walk away from this thing when your term in Congress ends; that you will be out there fighting along the way. I appreciate all the efforts that you have put forward.

I yield back.

Mr. ZELIFF. Thank you.

It has been a great partnership. I remember when we were down in Colombia, you and I went, at lunchtime we had a break, and rather than eating lunch we went and talked to all the DEA agents who were there risking their lives and thanking them on behalf of the Congress. There are a lot of people out there around the world that are fighting with very limited resources, and so the stakes are awfully high.

I thank you very much. It does take commitment, mostly because I have got three wonderful grandchildren and you have got a family that you are worried about, too. I think it's the future that we are worried about.

I guess I will jump into your comment there, that you kind of left. Wouldn't it have been great if we had that information available 4 months ago. And you sat right up there listening to 5 hours of testimony.

You know, where did you come out on all of this discussion, we heard it, we didn't hear it? It's 7—you know, it's 12 months in the making and now it's 7 months into it. We still don't have a final draft, it's not ready, it is not a finished product, it's not prime time.

I mean, if I were listening to all of this from the private sector, I would probably go nuts. But what do you think?

Mr. SNITCH. I spent some time running studies for the National Academy of Sciences and we ran into some of these same problems where you get draft, after draft, after draft. It comes to a point in time where you have got to fish or cut bait, and it's time to put some closure to a study.

Again, I think you could make an argument—and many of the criticisms of this report I think are valid, where you can probably analyze this to death. You can continue on. If there's enough money coming to the folks who are doing the study, they can keep analyzing and looking at new factors, new variables, almost ad infinitum.

I think what you have to do is get a study that is fairly well-focused, bring some conclusions to the table, let people discuss them, beat them around. If, indeed, they are nonsense and garbage, well, then they will be dismissed. If not, analyze them.

I think the important issue is to get the information and to get the ideas out on the table so people can have the ability to give and take and either agree with them or disagree with them. So the—I am not going to argue that the study should have been released earlier, but there gets to a point in time where decisions have to be made about how many drafts do you do and when does it become released to the public?

I would also say that it perhaps might have been useful in some of these earlier stages, if they could have consulted with the Congress, knowing full well that you were involved in some of these policy and budgetary issues, to say here is a study coming down the road which is going to raise some flags, because it does contradict certain approaches that we now take. And I think it probably would have been useful for you to see that, even if the document hadn't been publicly released.

Mr. ZELIFF. Especially since we are part of the partnership that gives them the resources that do what they do.

Mr. SNITCH. Most definitely.

Mr. REUTER. Mr. Chairman, could I comment?

Mr. ZELIFF. Sure.

Mr. REUTER. I think this is a document that is far too flimsy to be released. I have never seen peer review comments as totally damning as these ones, and I do not think this is a study that can be rescued. The conclusions are not supported and it would not indeed have been helpful in your deliberations. It is a study which having been reviewed has been found wanting in almost every relevant dimension.

Mr. ZELIFF. Well, there certainly is some strong disagreement with what you just said, and we have—that's one nice thing about democracy. We still don't have it resolved whether it was adequate research or whether it wasn't.

Mr. REUTER. There is a peer review process.

Mr. ZELIFF. The fact it was covered up or whether it wasn't. So we will have to go and solve that on another day.

I do have—on three pieces of the conclusions, I would like to ask you a few questions, Dr. Snitch, how you feel. And the first one is, continued counternarcotics efforts have significantly reduced the scope of the cocaine epidemic as compared to the levels that would have resulted had the cocaine trade continued to operate unimpeded. Yes or no?

Mr. SNITCH. I would think that would go without saying.

Mr. ZELIFF. OK. Second, when pursued with aggressive focused actions, source-zone interdiction efforts aimed at denial of production and transportation from the coca-growing regions have consistently caused marked increases in the street price of cocaine. This suggests that a long-term denial strategy could have lasting effects on the cocaine market. Yes or no?

Mr. SNITCH. Could I make two insertions? It has caused marked temporary increases in the street price. If you look there, there are peaks and valleys. So it has not been a long-term, but has caused a temporary.

Mr. ZELIFF. And probably the reason is that they have started into a 3-month effort and then stopped it because of funding?

Mr. SNITCH. Perhaps. It could be. I would say that the long-term denial strategy, if it was continuous, that is not stop and go, could lead—could have a lasting effect as opposed to episodic interdiction efforts that cause minor spikes.

Mr. ZELIFF. The last one would be, widely circulated analyses that have included a very low cost-effectiveness for source-owned interdiction, particularly as compared with treatment programs for heavy users, are counter to the empirical evidence. The discrepancy is largely attributed to the use and such analysis of improper measures of source-zone interdiction effectiveness, unrealistic assumptions regarding the margin of costs of large-scale additional treatments and reliance upon a questionable model to fit cocaine demand as a primary evaluation tool.

Mr. SNITCH. Well, I don't know if I would agree with that because I haven't studied and gone over the RAND report. I would say that the RAND study was not an improper measure of source-zone interdiction. It was a different measure. They were looking at different things.

The IDA study is a supply study that is looking at interdictions in a zone outside the United States. The RAND study appears to be looking at seizures within the United States.

If you had a very effective interdiction effort in Latin America and you cut off the supply of cocaine to the United States down to zero, if measured by the RAND criteria, there would be no seizures and, therefore, you have a very ineffective policy. So they are measuring apples and oranges here.

Mr. ZELIFF. All right. Mr. Reuter—Dr. Snitch, Dr. Reuter, thank you very much for your testimony. We appreciate your being here. Thank you.

[Whereupon, at 3:30 p.m., the subcommittee was adjourned.]

○